Voice Power

Voice Power

Joan Kenley, Ph.D.

An Owl Book

Henry Holt and Company
New York

*This book is dedicated
to my clients;
they have given
the core life to my work.*

Copyright © 1988 by Joan Kenley
All rights reserved, including the right to reproduce
this book or portions thereof in any form.
Published by Henry Holt and Company, Inc.,
115 West 18th Street, New York, New York 10011.
Published in Canada by Fitzhenry & Whiteside Limited,
195 Allstate Parkway, Markham, Ontario L3R 4T8.

Library of Congress Cataloging-in-Publication Data
Kenley, Joan.
Voice power / Joan Kenley.—1st Owl book ed.
p.   cm.
"An Owl book."
"First published in hardcover by Dodd, Mead & Company, Inc.,
in 1988"—T.p. verso.
Includes index.
ISBN 0-8050-1185-4 (pbk.)
1. Voice—Psychological aspects.   2. Mind and body.   I. Title.
BF637.V64K46   1989
153.6—dc20   89–7470
                                                              CIP

Henry Holt books are available at special discounts
for bulk purchases for sales promotions, premiums,
fund-raising, or educational use. Special editions
or book excerpts can also be created to specification.

For details contact:

Special Sales Director
Henry Holt and Company, Inc.
115 West 18th Street
New York, New York 10011

First published in hardcover by
Dodd, Mead & Company, Inc., in 1988.
First Owl Book Edition—1989

Printed in the United States of America
1   3   5   7   9   10   8   6   4   2

With special thanks to
Jerry Ackerman,
whose enormous contribution
made this book possible.

Contents

Contents

Acknowledgments

Over the years, I have been fortunate to meet and work with a constellation of people who have shaped both my life and my work. It would be impossible to name them all here, but I carry my past associations, and the understanding they have brought to me, as tangible gifts that open new insights as each day enfolds.

My deep gratitude and appreciation go to:

Ora Witte, Eleanor Phelps, and Betty Cashman, three outstanding women whose teaching and coaching provided the foundation for my voice training and eventual discoveries, and who shared their special techniques and understanding with me, and helped me at key stages of my career.

Dr. A.H. Almaas and Faisal Muqaddam, whose Diamond Approach for self-realization underlies many of the discussions of energetic and vocal aliveness in this book.

Dr. Ray Biase, whose professional generosity greatly aided my early investigations.

Drs. Clinton and Clifton Kew, whose psycho-spiritual counseling in the early days of my various careers started me on the road to self-discovery.

My precious parents, John and Lucy Kiess, for their abundance of love and understanding. And the relatives who have always been there for me in every way.

David Boadella and Myron Sharaf, two leaders in the neo-Reichian field whose writings, workshops, and personal teachings have added much to my work.

Eleanor Friede, my long-time friend who added her valuable expertise in the production of this book and who had the strength and vision to guide it from a dream to a reality, through many stages of frustration, difficulty, and finally completion; and Cynthia Vartan, my editor at Dodd, Mead for her recognition of this book's merits and her sharp editorial eye which greatly enhanced this book.

Byron Brown for his help with the BodyVoice Evaluation questionnaires, Peter Young for his art direction and computer graphics, and Kim Lincoln and Thaddeus Golas, graduates of the Kenley Method who agreed to demonstrate the techniques for the photographs in this book.

Ann Brebner, friend and professional mentor, who recently has co-led Master Film Acting Classes with me, where together we have shared in some of the personal discoveries described in this book.

Shirley Nelson, Roxanne Mankin, Don Carlson, Dr. Susan Ricketson, Jean Byrd, Joan Spangler, Dan Goff, and Sharon Solfvin, each for their own particular wonderful support and encouragement.

Special thanks and love to Maggi Thrall who was there on a daily basis to give advice, support, and friendship.

Finally, my special appreciation to Alain Gauthier, who tested the written word as a vehicle for my vocal techniques, and whose love and presence added much joy to the completion of this book.

Part 1

BodyVoice Discoveries

one

The BodyVoice Connection

How aware are you of the sound of your own voice?

If right now you were to say out loud, "Hello, how are you?" what qualities would you hear in your voice? What do you think other people would hear?

Would your business associates hear a relaxed, confident sound that puts them at ease and tells them you're ready for business?

Would your friends hear a voice that reflects how you're doing and how you feel about yourself?

You might be like Steve, who had the makings of a good company president, but whose boring voice detracted from his effectiveness as a leader. Or like Sharon, whose power in local politics was weakened by her nervousness at the podium. Or Martha, whose tentative-sounding voice was not taken seriously by her children. Or you might be like Don, whose skills as an organizational manager were often underrated because he became choked up when he wanted to be persuasive and then couldn't say what he meant.

This is the era of *personal* communication. In a world of rapid technological and economic changes, more than ever it's the power to communicate your own positive human qualities, as well as information, that inspires people and energizes organizations. Effective personal communication is as important to your aspirations, your relationships, and your self-expression as any hard-earned knowledge or technical skill. Yet it may also be the frontier of personal development you've overlooked.

Is your communication style an ally or an adversary in your

3

striving for personal achievement? If you aren't sure, it may be time to find out.

Your overall impact involves the kind of physical energy you communicate and the sound of your voice. In fact, in communicating feelings and attitudes *the sound of your voice can have more than five times the impact of what you say.*[1]

If you are unaware of how you sound, you may be relying exclusively on your *words* to communicate your personal qualities. The knowledge that you are sincerely engaged in the adventure of living, that you have a valuable contribution of energy and involvement to make to the world, that you are someone to be enjoyed and respected—these are internal experiences of your own personal energy that make you feel good about yourself. If you can communicate these qualities effectively, people will want to work with you, take you seriously, and spend time with you. This kind of communication happens primarily *without* words.

The sound of your speaking voice is one of the most important channels you have for communicating these nonverbal messages. Your vocal quality can reveal who you are directly, spontaneously, and powerfully whenever you speak. Or it can hide your individuality so that no one can sense who you really are, and even you aren't sure how much of you is behind what you say. By developing your vocal quality as part of a unity that includes your voice, breath, and body, you can discover many untapped resources for vitality, strength, and confidence.

The ancient Japanese culture had a tradition of honoring the sound of the voice. They felt that the voice revealed the person and how far a person's words could be trusted in his business and personal dealings. The *Hara-goe,* or voice from the lower belly, was more respected than a voice produced only by the throat. A voice coming from the lower abdomen was "valued as an expression of integrated wholeness and total presence,"[2] and was deserving of trust. A voice coming only from the larynx was considered insincere.

The same insight can be found in modern Western psychology. A person whose mind is very highly trained, but whose lower body instinctual energies are suppressed, often has confused, unclear emotional responses. But a person who acts from the body's natural

[1] Albert Mehrabian, *Silent Messages* (Belmont, Cal.: Wadsworth Publishing Company, Inc., 1971), p. 44.
[2] K.G. Von Durckheim, *Hara, The Vital Centre of Man* (London: George Allen & Unwin, Ltd., 1970), p. 53.

energy is in contact with emotion and instinct, and his body, voice, and personality are all parts of a unitary whole.[3]

David Rogers, author and marketing consultant, expresses some of the excitement of this perspective when he discusses one of the secrets of the samurai warrior—summoning the body energy known as *ki* or *chi*. Freed from negative thinking, focused, and breathing properly,

> . . . the samurai was able to perform extraordinary feats by directing his *ki* into . . . physical power. . . . This fed amazing power into his sword stroke, just as today it enables martial artists to break slabs of wood, brick and stone, and just as it will enable you to increase your power of action, whatever that action is—be it making a sales presentation, having a good time at a party or handling situations in day-to-day life.[4]

Rogers goes on to describe the experience of this body energy as "a personal force that you communicate to other people." It can come across as optimism, warmheartedness, self-confidence, courage, positive chemistry, or charisma.

Communication of your personal energy is vital for your health, well-being, and self-expression. But exactly how is it communicated? To a great extent, it is communicated by your vocal quality. With what I call the Kenley Method, you will have a simple, easy-to-learn way to bring the special facets of your energetic aliveness into the sound of your voice. Steve did, and his voice was no longer boring or an obstacle to his rise to company president. Sharon, too, learned to bring confidence to her voice and to take command of her political meetings. Martha discovered her tone of natural parental authority which children need and respect. And Don found that improving the sound of his voice was an effective way to increase his persuasiveness.

Voice and Body: A Unity

As you read this book, you will meet again and again the idea that the sound of your voice is inseparable from the energetic life

---

[3] Ron Kurtz and Hector Prestera, M.D., *The Body Reveals* (New York: Harper & Row/ Quicksilver Books, 1976), p. 4.

[4] David J. Rogers, *Fighting To Win* (Garden City, N.Y.: Doubleday and Company, 1984), pp. 72-73.

and breath of your entire body. This idea originates from two sources.

The first is the work of the many psychologists, philosophers, scientists, and healers who have helped us learn to see mind and body as a unity. From the ancient Yogic and Tantric traditions to the work of Wilhelm Reich to the findings of modern psychology and physiology, there has emerged a consensus of understanding that thinking, feeling, and doing are intimately connected with the flow of natural body energies—with a healthy way of breathing as the indispensable foundation for experiencing this connection.

The second source is my own personal experience as a performer, voice consultant, and psychologist. In my work, each day provides fresh examples of how completely the voice is part of the mind-body unity. A truly personal vocal quality is not a matter of expert vocabulary or schooled articulation. It comes from breathing fully, and from educating your body to greater sensitivity and aliveness. It comes from experiencing your body from head to toe as a unified field of vitality for the harmonious interplay of breath, emotion, and sound. Emotional understanding and body awareness play a much greater role than mechanical vocal gymnastics in helping people discover and develop a dynamic personal voice.

In a recent interview, actor Jack Nicholson revealed how the method he uses to warm up his voice is based on just the kind of harmony of breath, emotion, and sound inherent in the exercises I have developed as part of the Kenley Method. He sings a nursery rhyme while his arms hang limply at his sides, his shoulders droop, his jaw is slack, and his face is drained of expression. The sound comes out deep, resonant, and uninflected. The point of this warm-up, said Nicholson, "is to get the physical body, the emotional body and the mental body into neutral. Then you should be able to hear through the voice what's actually happening inside. . . . It's a way of locating the tensions, the tiny tensions . . . that get in the way of getting into a role."[5]

If you've never thought about your voice and your body as important to *your* professional and personal roles, you're in for some exciting discoveries. Ahead of you is the realization that not only your diaphragm, but your lower torso and legs play an essential role in supporting your breath, and giving your voice added strength

[5] Ron Rosenblum, "Acting: The Creative Mind. The Method & Mystique of Jack Nicholson," *The New York Times*, (July 13, 1986). Copyright © 1986 by The New York Times Company. Reprinted by permission.

that can release much of the tension and stress that may be part of the way you speak. You will discover that the desirable qualities you want in your voice—colorful intonation and phrasing, persuasiveness, conviction, sincerity—do not come from mechanically memorizing endless techniques of voice production. Certain basics are necessary, but real effectiveness in correcting or enhancing your vocal quality is achieved by releasing your breath, body, and voice so that your natural instincts and emotional impulses can organically shape the style of your communication.

Take a moment and ask yourself these questions:

Do you think of the sound of your speaking voice as something just there to be taken for granted, or as a personal resource that can be developed to help you achieve a richer, fuller life?

Does it make sense to you that there is a precise, direct connection between free-flowing body energies and a dynamic voice?

Are you ready to explore how your body's sexual energies can bring aliveness to your voice?

Do you realize that having an inner relationship with your more subtle body sensations can add more of who you are to what you say—to friends, lovers, and business associates?

One day recently, Maria, an accounting whiz, with a pleasantly round face and figure, sat in my office, unburdening herself about her voice. It was flat, she said, and expressed no color or energy. An associate had finally told her that if he had to judge by the sound of her voice, he'd think she was bored to death with her job and her career. Perhaps equally upsetting, her lover kept asking her if she was tired of their relationship, and her efforts to reassure him all seemed to backfire. She was sure now that the sound of her voice was the culprit. She wanted to get some life into her voice, make it expressive, enthusiastic, vivacious.

In order to diagnose the lack of energy in Maria's voice, I began by asking her questions to sensitize her to the need for an awareness of her body. A dynamic voice originates from a certain body aliveness, and if the body is low on energy, the reasons for this lack of vitality must be checked.

"What do you feel?" I asked her. "Are you aware of any identifiable sensations in your arms and legs? In your chest and lower torso?"

After a few moments of making the unfamiliar effort to focus on specific body sensations, Maria admitted, "Not very much."

Maria realized that her body was like a stranger to her. She did not have a very strong or conscious relationship with her inner sensory nature. I could see this manifested in her shallow breathing and general lack of physical and emotional charge. Maria was living her life on a low-energy flame, and this was revealed clearly in the colorless sound of her voice.

To help Maria's voice, I helped her begin to experience her body. For the next six weeks, she went through the various stages of the Kenley Method. Her breathing deepened, and she learned what it was like to feel energy flowing in her body. And as the experience of this personal energy became accessible, she began to feel more and more truly alive.

In the third week she had her first breakthrough. It was a simple enough event: as she practiced her breathing, she began to feel the welcome sensation of energy in her lower torso.

"What is it?" I asked.

"It's like . . . a flutter," she said. "It feels kind of . . . alive!"

And as she described that small first flutter of body aliveness, I could hear the beginning of a new aliveness in the sound of her voice.

Your BodyVoice

Because body and voice are a unity, I refer to them as one: your BodyVoice. You can tell when you've found your BodyVoice by the way you sound and the way you feel.

Your BodyVoice is your personal sound. It is never lacking in emotional expressiveness. Once you learn how to use your Body-Voice, you will have a vocal sound that is filled with the richness of your inner life, expressive of your joys, sorrows, angers and enthusiasms.

Your BodyVoice is confident and steady even when you are in stressful situations. You may have an entire roomful of people anticipating your presentation, or that special customer who holds the purse strings waiting for your big idea, but your BodyVoice has the power and energy of your entire body to sustain you in spite of the pressure.

The one thing I consider most characteristic of people who have developed their BodyVoice is that the sounds of their voices are filled with that quality we call charisma. Their voices are alive and make you feel, as powerfully as a physical touch, that person's genuine individual presence. Long after the conversation, speech, or performance is over, you can still hear and feel the impact of the person. We all know what it's like to look into a pair of eyes and feel we are seeing right into someone's soul. We know how it feels when someone enters the room and their energy immediately enlivens and gladdens us. These experiences of charisma can also be felt in the sound of *your* BodyVoice.

A Voice to Remember

Your BodyVoice is a voice to remember. Newscaster Linda Ellerbee has such a voice. Like the best journalists of radio and television, she shares with you her personal connection to the news and the commitment she brings to her role. The sound of her voice expresses the enjoyment she has in the telling of and the caring for what she brings into your home.

Maya Angelou, author, poet, and performer, has a voice that brings her world alive. When you listen to her read from her books, you feel that no part of her is inaccessible. From the fluidity of her body to the resonance of her voice, you know that you are experiencing her authentic being, communicated in all of her emotion and depth. Whether she is relating the terror of her early childhood sexual abuse or the joys of her many experiences, you feel that she is not withholding anything, and her voice continues to speak to you long after you're once again immersed in your own life.

If you have watched the television series "Hotel" or seen the film *All About Eve*, you know that actress Anne Baxter had a voice that made all of the emotions she portrayed accessible to you. Even without watching the screen you could experience her involvement in her character and connect with her emotions. The sound of her voice alone created that living presence. And if you think about it, much of the tribute we pay to actors such as Richard Burton, Don Ameche, and Raymond Burr is because of their outstanding voices.

Oprah Winfrey, actress, talk show host, and entrepreneur, has an emotional and body sense and vocal sound that communicate her eminently human and sensitive qualities. From her touching performance in *The Color Purple* to her down-to-earth TV hosting, she exemplifies a communicator to whom we can all respond. Walter Cronkite will be remembered as one of the greatest voices of television news. His clear, crisp, fatherly baritone seemed made to carry us through the fastbreaking, tumultuous events of this century. Perhaps more than anyone else's, his voice embodied immediacy, excitement, and trust.

It's the expression of an integrated wholeness of emotion and physical aliveness that gives these voices their life, individuality, and charisma, and makes them so unforgettable. Meryl Streep's voice is not especially deep or resonant, but there is no doubt that it plumbs a place within her where her emotions are accessible and that she communicates those intimate emotions to her movie audiences. Similarly, Robert Mitchum, Jessica Lange, and Diane Sawyer have memorable voices, not because of any isolated quality, but because they evoke such a strong sense of personal individual presence.

The voices of Winston Churchill and John F. Kennedy live on in the memories of all who heard them. When Kennedy spoke, his voice was connected to his passionate conviction that America could create a land of justice and equality. The sound of his voice carried a nation's aspirations and ideals. You may have only heard Kennedy speak in historic TV or film clips, but even so, the sound of his voice is as present as if he had just stepped before the cameras to address the nation. His voice still holds a spellbinding power.

Churchill, too, had a voice that mobilized a nation. There was a voice whose sound even now seems synonymous with courage, fortitude, the anger of conviction, and an entire people's indomitable will to survive. Try to imagine Churchill's famous speeches during the dark days of World War II spoken by someone with a less commanding, less impassioned voice. It was the *felt* experience of Churchill's voice that carried his words and made him the acknowledged spokesman of his people.

In Search of Your Voice

Some people are born with magnificent voices, just as some people are born athletes or born musicians. Others have to develop their vocal sound, but they are no less effective for having had to learn how to find a personal vocal quality.

Everyone has the potential to develop a BodyVoice, and that means you can have a speaking voice with charisma. Until you start making this discovery, your voice may exhibit any of a number of problems with tension, fatigue, or control. A lackluster vocal quality, short on aliveness and expressiveness, is commonly caused by a lack of connection with your body and its energies. Overreliance on the muscles of your throat, as if they alone were responsible for producing your vocal sound and pronouncing your words, can lead to fatigue and hoarseness. If you talk in your throat when you are tense or under stress, your throat will not have the strength or capacity to support your voice, and your sound may quiver or become tight and high-pitched. Denied access to the strength of the body, you may have problems with speaking too fast or too slow, too soft or too loud.

The most characteristic thing about people whose voices are cut off from their bodies is how unaware of the sound of their voices they are. If you're happy at a victory or promotion, and want to be sure you're sharing that feeling of joy with someone you love, can you tell if that joy is expressed in the sound of your voice? Do you have a characteristic way you try to get feeling in your voice? How can you know if you do?

A researcher in nonverbal communication once asked a number of people to say something sarcastic. Many of the subjects relied unconsciously on their facial expressions, and when tapes of the experiment were played back, there was not a hint of sarcasm in the sound of their voices. If they had been with friends, hoping to reach out by expressing anger or humor, they would not have succeeded very well, and might have felt rejected or misunderstood.

The first step in overcoming these kinds of problems and developing your BodyVoice is to be sure you understand that you cannot get a dynamic, personal sound for your speaking voice without contacting the energetic life of your entire body.

David's voice used to be a stumbling block but now has earned him well-deserved rewards. He began to think about his voice when his new position required him to make frequent public presentations. Noticing his difficulty in holding his audience's attention, he assumed his voice was not doing its job. His problem was that his voice was swallowed up by tension in his throat. But in David's estimation, all he needed was a quick fix.

"Joan," he said, "I'm busy. I work in a high-pressure job. I'm used to meeting impossible deadlines and doing things 'quick and dirty' when I need to. Just give me the basics. I'm sure it's just a matter of giving me a few pointers."

I told him, "What you really need is to project a strong sense of personal connection with what you say to an audience. You want people to respond to your energy, your enthusiasm for your job, your commitment and conviction. We need to look at certain emotional qualities that you could experience more thoroughly. Something is blocking these feelings from finding their natural expression in both your body and your voice. Relaxation will be the first step to help you get in touch with more of your emotional life."

I smiled as I added, "This won't be 'quick and dirty.' But it's what will really help you in the long run."

And, in fact, as David's work with me progressed, and his voice became more flexible and expressive, he stopped looking for a quick fix. Instead, he began to appreciate the value of a deeper process of self-discovery. He learned that by relaxing his body, he not only relaxed his throat but released his natural expressiveness. He felt more alive and aware, and his voice became an extension of the new, more confident way he approached his life and work. The impact of his presentations soon improved, and he no longer lost his audience.

Your Voice: Friend or Foe?

Take a moment to think about what the discovery of your BodyVoice can do for you. You may not have considered what an essential part the sound of your voice plays in your self-expression, or how your BodyVoice can help you become a dynamic communicator.

Many people come to me for help with their voice only after they have worked on all the other parts of their packaging—their grooming, dress, hair, weight, skin, and so forth. They have read all the books on how to build the right business wardrobe for professional advancement, how to cope with the realities of intimate relationships, or how to practice aikido on their inner demons. But they have neglected their voices, sometimes because they did not realize what a powerful impression the voice makes on others, and sometimes because they did not think there was any way that their vocal quality could be changed.

Roberta, an up-and-coming manager in her mid-thirties, with a flair for high-tech marketing, is a good example. She was an energetic, bright redhead determined to get the most out of life. She had worked diligently on her professional appearance and style, on her health, and on her social and relationship skills. It wasn't until a new position required her to become directly involved in important meetings with her firm's customers that she suspected she had overlooked something. A meticulous organizer who could present arguments logically and had all the facts at her fingertips, she was prepared for each meeting, but somehow, she could tell that her real message was not being heard. The constructive dialogue she was supposed to encourage was not taking place.

Only gradually did it occur to Roberta that the problem was not her content, but the sound of her voice. When she finally called me, I could hear her problem right away over the phone: a harsh, strident quality that made people turn away irritated, even though what she was saying was well-planned and considerate.

As I worked with Roberta, it became clear that there were sides to her personality she was afraid to express. She'd always stopped herself from allowing her femininity and personal warmth to come through. She was afraid that she'd lose her effectiveness in the business world and never get ahead if she let this more personal side of her be part of her business life. Her father was a strong role model for her, a hard-driving unemotional businessman whose manner she tried to emulate.

What Roberta discovered with me was that there *was* an effective, practical way for her to change and enhance her voice. Developing greater awareness of her body energies was a key step. As the weeks went by, her awareness of her heart feelings and the more personal energies of her lower torso began to emerge. With the BodyVoice warm-up exercises, the sound of her voice changed, too. It became more colorfully alive and lost its hard, overbearing quality. To her surprise, by getting in touch with her softer side, she developed a much more richly communicative, professional-sounding voice.

But something else happened as well. As I mentioned, Roberta had been through almost every kind of self-improvement course— except one for her voice. Now, ironically, by developing a personal sound for her voice, she found the personal growth she'd been seeking. She learned how to balance the different sides of her nature and to achieve a fuller dimension of her own individual expression. She said to me later, "Joan, I had my doubts when you first hinted that my life was going to change. But that's just what's happened."

An awakening of this kind is not uncommon for people who

develop their voices by using my techniques, because the method for developing the BodyVoice is based on tapping fuller energies and releasing the body from its emotional blocks and inhibitions.

Your First Voice Impressions

Roberta waited a long time to seek help for her voice because she had not considered that how she sounded could be important to her self-growth and business success. This is a mistake you don't want to make.

As mentioned earlier, in communicating feelings and attitudes the sound of your voice is more than *five times* as important as what you say. In a classic study on the relative impact of facial expressions, vocal quality, and verbal messages, the following order of importance was found for verbal and nonverbal communications:

Face   55%
Voice   38%
Words   7%[6]

You can take advantage of this knowledge by not relying solely on your facial expressions or your words to carry the burden of your communication. Learning to make fuller use of the sound of your voice will increase your impact on others.

If you're like Roberta, you may not be aware of how your voice sounds or of the image that it may be creating in the minds of the people you know and work with.

When I speak to a new group about the Kenley Method, I use the following demonstration of the power that the voice has to create perceptions and opinions about the speaker. I simply ask the person introducing me to have the audience close their eyes before I begin my presentation. Then, from the back of the room, I introduce myself several times, each time changing the quality of my voice. I might caricature the voice of a drawling Southern belle, a nasal prude, an authoritarian teacher, or a breathy beauty queen.

The result of this demonstration is always the same. The audience is astonished to discover how quickly the quality of my

---

[6] Mehrabian, *Silent Messages*, p. 44.

voice conjures up strong images in their minds, and creates bizarre impressions before they see what I really look like. In fact, people who have only heard my voice on the phone often say that they picture me as a tall brunette, when actually I am a five-foot-three-inch blond.

Scientific studies have confirmed the reality of such impressions based on vocal quality:

> There is a widespread tendency for listeners to attribute specific personality characteristics to an individual on the basis of his speech. Audiences often derive their impressions of a lecturer from the sounds of his voice as well as from the words that he utters. It is customary for personnel managers to be influenced in their decisions by the voices of those they interview . . . In all these cases there is evidently an implicit assumption that the voice is, to some degree, a reflection of personality.[7]

The personality characteristics that people attribute based on the sound of the voice are more specific—and more accurate—than you might expect. Look at the following table for a generalized summary of how people tend to perceive the major types of vocal qualities.

Vocal Qualities and Perceived Personality Traits

Vocal Quality	Perceived Personality Traits
Breathy	Immaturity, childishness, sexiness. Can also convey softness, awe, lightness, love, passion, admiration.
Tense	Uncooperativeness, emotional insecurity, bad temper. Can make the listener tense. Can also signal anger, rudeness, frustration, cruelty.
Nasal	Dull, lazy, a whiner. Can also convey repugnance, boredom, complaint, self-deprecation.
Rounded	Idealistic, authoritarian, pompous. Can also suggest positiveness, expansiveness, importance.
Flat	Unemotional, unenthusiastic. Can also indicate laziness, boredom, displeasure.

[7] E. Mallory and V. Miller, "A Possible Basis for the Association of Voice Characteristics and Personality Traits," *Speech Monographs* 25 (1958): 255.

Thin	Immature, insecure, indecisive. Can also convey doubt, apology, weakness.
Throaty	Control, holding back, lack of emotional freedom. Can also convey caution, carefulness, and exacting attitudes.
Forward	Superciliousness, coldness, disdain. Can also convey precision, intellectual focus.

Based on discussions in *The Unspoken Dialogue* by Judee K. Burgoon and Thomas Saine (Boston: Houghton Mifflin Co., 1978).

Why the sound of your voice is so important to your overall impact is easy to understand when you consider the most essential things you need to communicate. True, we live in an information age and when we talk, it would seem that the emphasis is on the information we want to share. But when people meet to talk, the primary emphasis is on *nonverbal* social and cultural cues that are largely communicated by facial expressions, body gestures, and *the sound of the voice*.

In fact, your vocal quality is one of the primary channels of information for first impressions, attraction and liking, credibility, status and power, emotional messages, self-presentation, and change of attitudes and behavior. Interpersonal judgments on whether to approach or avoid someone, quick evaluations of dominance and submissiveness, and judgments of how responsive and interesting a person is, are made almost entirely on nonverbal cues. That means when someone is deciding whether they like you, think you are competent, wonder if they can intimidate you, or consider if you are worth knowing, they will rely significantly on the sound of your voice.

A Common Self-Deception

You can see now why it is so essential that you know what the sound of your voice is communicating to others. And you can understand why you need to discover your own truly personal sound—*your* BodyVoice.

Bob, a twenty-four-year-old computer salesman with whom I recently consulted, got something of a shock along these lines when he began to work with me. As far as Bob could tell, he was coming across in a positive, powerful way. When I asked him how effective his communication style was in his work situations, he said, "Meeting people and marketing myself—no problem."

Bob had a low, booming voice, and he equated its pitch and volume with the personal qualities he believed he was communicating. But despite its apparent power, Bob's vocal quality was ineffective because it was not connected to his body. His sound had a tight, controlled edge that made me feel uneasy in response to him.

"Bob, I don't think you're aware that you sound cautious and somewhat nervous," I told him.

This hit him pretty hard. All the time he thought he was being extremely composed and confident, he was actually giving the nonverbal message that he was guarded and uneasy. As Bob became more aware of his voice and his body, he realized how he had deceived himself. He had thought that merely having a loud voice was communicating a sense of power. The loud voice was his self-devised signal that he was doing all right. It had not occurred to him that he was out of touch with his body, or that a sense of power is something he could feel directly in his body and his voice.

A Day in the Life of Your Voice

As you begin to think about the sound of your voice and how it affects other people's perceptions of you, do not be discouraged. Every healthy person can overcome common vocal problems. You *can* change the sound of and enhance the quality of your voice. In fact, if you stop for a moment and think about how many kinds of vocal messages you send out each day, you will discover that you have the beginnings of developing a knowledgeable connection between your emotions and the way you sound. Let's imagine a day in the life of your voice, and see what and how it communicates.

When you wake up in the morning, you probably have an established routine you follow to get yourself out of bed, dressed, fed and off to work or on to your first household chores, child-care responsibilities, or errands. If you're like most people, you have a distinct and easily recognizable *Morning Voice* that you invariably use before you've had your first cup of coffee or become fully awake and ready for the day.

Your *Morning Voice* may not be very articulate. It may be some form of plaintive groaning whose purpose is to keep other people at bay until you've gotten yourself more together. One couple I know is perfectly willing to admit that at 7 A.M. he is a frog and she is a squeakbox. Nonetheless, their *Morning Voices* do the job of communicating to each other that they are awake, alive and well, and committed to facing the day.

When you arrive at work, it's time to say, "Good morning" to a great number of people and dive into whatever tasks, meetings, confrontations, or problems await you. You probably instinctively switch to your *Work Voice*. It might be a cheerful or cooperative sound, or a firm tone that says you're ready to roll up your shirt-sleeves or boot up your personal computer. Your *Work Voice* may be enthusiastic, friendly, or no-nonsense.

Your *Work Voice* may carry you through the day, but the moment your manager calls you in to give a pitch for your latest project or you realize it's time for your performance evaluation, you put on your *Up-and-Coming Voice*. This is how you talk when you want to sound positive, powerful, competent, brimming with bright ideas, and ready to take on all challenges. If you're like Bob, to convey power your *Up-and-Coming Voice* may be deliberately but inappropriately loud. On the other hand, you may have a sound that communicates eagerness, willingness to cooperate, or whatever else you know to be the most desirable professional quality at your company.

Some time in the afternoon, the phone rings. It's your husband, wife, boyfriend, or girlfriend. Busy as you are, you switch into your *Relationship Voice*, the voice you use to express your identity as a "special other." The conversation may be just to take a break, to hear the welcome sound of your lover's voice, to coordinate errands, or to doublecheck on your plans for the evening. But your *Relationship Voice*, if things are currently harmonious, will have a characteristic tone—happy, sweet, maybe even humorously facetious—that connects you and your partner to the world of love and sharing. As the Prince sings to Cinderella in Rossini's opera, "The sound of your voice is not unfamiliar to my heart."

If your day is spent primarily as a homemaker, or taking care of children, you probably have another entire set of voices: your *Parent Voice*, that complex combination of tones that indicates affection, attentiveness, and authority; your *P.T.A. Voice* of concern and involvement; your *Home Manager Voice* for directing the repair people, deliveries, and all the other myriad of personnel you must deal with to keep a household going.

When the day is over, you may be fatigued and feeling the pressures and worries of your life closing in on you. If someone talks to you, you respond in your *Tired Voice*, the voice you may use more often to talk to yourself about your worries than to another person. Worn out, closed down, ennervated—this may be your *Tired Voice*, and what it may really be communicating is that you're ready for a time-out and a hug.

As you can see, your voice already has the potential for emotional variety and expressiveness. But why stop here? Why not develop that potential, and allow your voice to be even more fully expressive in every part of your life?

Dr. Paul Ekman, a noted researcher in nonverbal communication, estimates that the human face has more than seven thousand combinations of muscle positions to communicate all the nuances of human emotion. Your voice is naturally just as variable, flexible, and extraordinary. When you speak, imagine that there could be seven thousand shadings of emotion in your vocal quality. If your voice is freely released, it has all the necessary potential to communicate the full range of your individuality.

The Entrepreneur: A Case History

Here is a good example of what happened when someone whose voice was cut off from his body learned to make the BodyVoice connection.

Mike is an entrepreneur whose work and life-style demand effective communication not just of plans and ideas, but of personal qualities. Inspiring trust and confidence between partners and customers is the essential first step in getting any entrepreneurial project off the ground. In Mike's world, a feeling that "I can work with this guy" is what makes or breaks every deal.

When I first met Mike, he had good communication skills and the potential for a gorgeous voice, naturally low and mellifluous. His problem, he said, was that when he wanted to speak with important clients, he became nervous and began to talk through his nose. As a result, his voice lost power and he did not come across effectively in critical meetings.

Like David, the busy client who wanted a quick fix, Mike first assumed that his problem was in the mechanics of voice production and that all he needed was a way to practice not talking through his nose.

"Mike," I observed, "you already know how to talk without that harsh, nasal tone. You do it most of the time. In fact, your voice sounds good right now."

"But it's not there when I need it," he said.

"Exactly. Your real problem is your nervousness in crucial situations and what that does to your voice. You need to connect your voice with the untapped strength of your body in order to gain more confidence. Our first task will be to discover why you're unable to make that connection to your body's energy."

For Mike, this way of looking at his voice was at first totally alien. He was not accustomed to thinking about this kind of energetic connection with his body. Even though he used strenuous workouts at the gym as a way to relieve frustrations, as far as feelings, sensations, and signals went, his body was a source of tension or— nothing. Although he did not fully understand it, he sensed a basic core of truth in what I said. His primary problem was emotional, and my description of his voice as "ungrounded" was exactly how he felt when he was nervous—as if he was treading in a sea of tension.

As we began to work on his voice, Mike became aware of himself as someone "living in his head." In fact, Mike was often lost in what I refer to as the human Bermuda Triangle.

"That's the triangle of tension formed by your head, neck, and shoulders," I explained to him. "It's where your experience of your body energies disappears. Both the awareness and the aliveness of your body, from your toes to your chest, vanish right into that tension trap in your upper body. Then the body energies you really need to communicate fully disappear, too."

We discovered that the high level of tension Mike experienced was related to problems with self-esteem. Although he was handsome, accomplished, and articulate, he was driven by an overwhelming need to prove his worth. No matter what he was doing, his energy was tied up in an unrelenting, self-critical interior dialogue that went on continuously in his mind. Was he working hard enough? Was he accomplishing enough? Was he giving his business the devotion it deserved?

Mike's need to prove his worth by self-punishing discipline led him to take extraordinary measures. He was an avid music lover, but he wouldn't permit himself to have a car radio or tape deck. He felt this would distract him from concentrating on business matters as he drove each day from his home to his office. I was not surprised, however, when Mike told me that what really happened during his commute time was an angry argument with himself about what wasn't going right in his business, what difficult clients were making him miserable, and what things seemed wrong about his life. It was also not surprising that, living in this mental jungle, Mike had no way to bring power and confidence into his voice.

My direction with Mike was to help him explore his body emotionally and learn that there was a lot more that could go on inside him than "tension or—nothing." He learned how to listen to his body and identify exactly where he was tense and what that tension felt like. This exploration of his body led to a process of self-understanding. He began to recognize the irritated anger he directed at others as a reflection of the critical anger he directed at himself. The grip of tension on his body seemed to him now a measure of how incredibly hard on himself he was, and of how much he needed to allow compassion for himself and others to operate in his thinking and actions. With this recognition and the exercises he was using, he began to release these negative behavior patterns and to experience his body as a source of confidence and strength.

We discovered that some of Mike's problem with self-esteem came from the verbal abuse he had received from his father and his teachers. Significantly enough, it was not only their critical words he remembered, but the caustic, contemptuous tone of their voices which had etched their put-downs so deeply and lastingly in his memory and with such punishing power in the unconscious reactions of his body. The damage done by "vocal abuse" is often worse than some forms of physical abuse because it becomes such an invisible but dominating part of a person's character.

Initially, it was hard for Mike to relax and let go of his negative thinking. He was afraid that his life would fall apart if he didn't constantly worry about it. But as he began to feel what it was like to release his body, things fell into place for him. He could see where to look within himself for his emotional resources.

"When I have a meeting scheduled and I'm feeling nervous," he realized, "it's that alive, grounded feeling that I want to get into my voice."

As he progressed, it was exciting to watch the change. The focus of his identity shifted from that self-punishing mental dialogue to the growing sense of aliveness in his body, and his true individuality began to emerge. You could hear the difference in his voice. The more in touch with his body Mike became, the more relaxed, confident, and expressive his voice became. He now knew what it was like to feel a natural, spontaneous sense of self-esteem, and how to allow that inner worth to express itself through his voice.

I had worked with Mike to help him feel the energies in his chest, lower torso, and legs. One day, he phoned me to say he had just come from a meeting where he'd felt powerfully in charge and had landed a large account he'd been seeking.

"When you spoke at the meeting, where did you feel your voice coming from?" I asked.

"Everywhere," he laughed, "like a tympani reverberating throughout my entire body."

There couldn't be a better way to say that he had made the full BodyVoice connection.

Mike continues to be successful, and to make his success more emotionally enriching. The company he founded has really taken off, and he's enjoying his ability to express more of his individuality in his work and in the sound of his voice.

A Personal Story: The Burglar

I have a story of my own about my BodyVoice and how it may have saved my life.

A few years ago, a burglar broke into my apartment. Apparently he had staked out my place, watched me leave, then karate-kicked my door open. Unexpectedly for him, I had forgotten something and returned a few minutes later. I found my door frame splintered.

A strong hot energy filled my body. I was so angry, I didn't stop to think about the jeopardy I might be in. I stormed into my living room, and when I saw the intruder's shadow in the hallway, I yelled, "Get in here!" He came out from my bedroom, and I raged at him, "Did you take anything?"

All I could think of was that if he had, he should give it back. I don't know what I expected to happen, but believe it or not, he stood there, hung his head like a bad child, and creaked out a raspy, "No."

My fury peaked as I boomed out in a loud, deep BodyVoice: "GET OUT!"

And he immediately ran through the door.

By the time the police arrived, my emotions had cooled down and I realized the danger I had faced with such bravado. Instinctively, my voice had become a weapon, and the burglar had felt that power. Last year, I read that "CBS Evening News" anchor Dan Rather had a similar experience. A housebreaker at his vacation home fled when Rather shouted him out.

Of course I don't recommend that you confront an intruder in this way. But the spontaneous strength and power that surged through my body and voice during those moments comes from an energy source that you could find useful for your own voice. It's the BodyVoice you evoke to stop a child from touching a hot stove or running into the street, or when you must communicate justifiable anger or impress others with your determination.

Introduction to the Kenley Method

In this chapter we've seen some of the ways that enhancing the sound of your voice can make an important difference in your life. As you read the rest of this book, you'll make the following additional discoveries:

Breathing correctly to develop your BodyVoice will also improve your overall health, energy, and maybe even your longevity.

Releasing your BodyVoice will release and eliminate feelings of stress. And the technique for reducing tension is fast, effective, and portable.

Developing your BodyVoice can have a positive effect on your sexual/ energetic aliveness and your personal attractiveness.

Your vocal history of family dynamics and early childhood experience can reveal more than you might expect about the acquired characteristics and inhibitions of your current vocal quality and communication style.

Just as you would do a physical warm-up before running a race, you can do a vocal warm-up before giving a speech, going on a date, or making a sales call.

Grounding your voice in your lower body will eliminate chronic hoarseness, help you sound more powerful, and give you more confidence when talking on the phone.

You can have a vocal quality that reflects the way you feel inside. How you sound needs to be in step with the person you've become in your own self-exploration. Your voice can have a warm, adult, fully personal sound.

To educate your voice, you must educate your ear. You can become aware of how people perceive the sound of your voice, and learn to hear more in the sound of other people's voices.

Releasing your body, breath, and voice will help you develop your awareness of certain body energies that can increase your self-sufficiency, compassion, creativity, and mental clarity more than you might have imagined possible.

The techniques presented in this book come from my personal experience and over ten years of work with performers and professionals. I am delighted to be able to share with you my own discovery of the BodyVoice concept and the development of the Kenley Method.

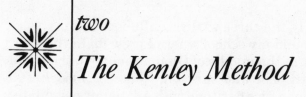

two

The Kenley Method

Whenever I think back on my career, it always surprises me in some ways that I've ended up a communication specialist teaching people to use their voices more effectively, when I began as an actress. But then, it all makes sense, too. It reflects my lifelong involvement and fascination with the voice. Along the way, I've done a lot of what is called "voiceover" work—the unseen person or narrator you hear when you don't see someone speaking on screen, or all the voices you hear on radio advertisements. I've been the voice for commercials, industrial films, video presentations, slide shows, even a synthesized computer chip. I've also watched with excitement the changes in technology for working with the voice, from the days when portable tape recorders weighed too much to carry them more than a few blocks, to the present age of audio and video cassettes.

I had problems with my voice and much to learn about myself and my emotional life, and how it affected my body, before I discovered my BodyVoice. The story of that discovery reflects the kind of process you may go through in changing your life as you discover your own vocal history and the emotional and body energy changes that accompany true vocal improvement. When I started out in life, filled with the ambition to be an actress and make a place for myself in the world, I had very little idea of the connection between my voice and my emotional life and body. As I attempted to train my voice for my career, I went through many phases.

The Quest for My Voice

I remember clearly the three earliest influences on my voice: my father, my mother, and my school where I grew up in the small town of Bucyrus, right in the middle of Ohio. From my father, John Kiess, a general practitioner and surgeon, I had the model of an expressive voice. His was a nice baritone with a dynamic personality and the sureness I wanted to emulate. Since he was usually so busy, I didn't have a chance to have many intimate conversations with him. But I remember when we had family dinners and friends or relatives came over, my father would sit at the head of the table as if he were a king holding court. His voice was colorful and his stories so entertaining that everyone admired him, especially me. My mother Lucy's voice, on the other hand, was soft and quiet, communicating her somewhat shy, but very sweet nature.

I also had picked up certain regional accents. During the war years, my father was head of an Army hospital in South Carolina, and I learned to talk with a Southern accent. I was precocious in some ways and had a good vocabulary, so even at age three I was allowed to answer the phone, which I did with a Southern drawl—"Dahkter Keeze's rezidance." To my family and their friends, I was already a bit of a character. Then, back in Ohio by age five, I began to acquire Midwestern speech patterns. I didn't realize I had an accent until years later when a theater professor told me I should work to get rid of it.

"What are you talking about?" I asked.

He pointed out that I said "git" instead of "get," "jist" instead of "just," and "warsh" instead of "wash." Later, when I took singing lessons, some teachers thought I was off-key because I had certain inflections for some of the vowels: "day-ee," "may-ee." When I learned to stop stretching the words and could sing "day" as one syllable, "deh," I got back on pitch.

When I was a schoolgirl dreaming of acting on the stage, I had my own secret image of how my voice should sound. Every Saturday I went with my grandfather to one of the two movie theaters in town. I always wanted to go to the one that played Superman serials and Gene Autry and Roy Rogers movies. When I played cowboys and Indians with my older brother and his friends, I wanted to be accepted. I wanted to be seen and heard. So I ran after them, dreaming of owning a pony and starring with Gene Autry or Roy Rogers, and I always made sure I was loud enough, hoping my voice would help make me one of the guys. It was not a very sophisticated approach to enhancing my vocal quality, but it was my first encounter with the issues of vocal power that I would later find of general concern to the people I worked with and those I've helped with their self-development.

I had wanted to be an actress since I was five or six years old, and I took the lead in most of the grammar school plays. One of my more interesting critical acclaims was for imitating the sound of a chicken in the seventh grade class play—clearly I was ready to take on the challenge of even the most demanding roles. I had a strong voice that carried well. In fact, I could always be heard clearly in the back of any auditorium or theater. This also helped me to get elected cheerleader. Being a cheerleader was just another way to perform for an audience, and I loved it. But I was perturbed because I never got hoarse. I thought it sounded wonderful when the other girls would lose their voices after a game. To me a husky voice sounded sexy.

Then, when I was 15, I attended the University of Colorado at Boulder young actors' summer training and performance program, where I was voted Best Actress. Three years later, at Mildred Dunnock's Barnard Summer Theatre actor's apprentice program in New York City, I was voted Most Promising Actress by the professional faculty. However, there was still a part of me that was insecure about my craft, my talents, and career decisions. I flipflopped between feeling destined for greatness and feeling doomed to failure. You may have had periods in your own life where in a whirl of excitement, competition, accomplishments, and insecurities, it was difficult to think about yourself objectively. This was true for me regarding my acting and especially my voice, which I was committed to improving until it was the wonderful, deeply moving voice of a fine actress.

Working on my voice turned out to be a fascinating, yet often frustrating experience. This was an era when most methods of teaching the singing or speaking voice involved mainly verbal instruction. I remember going to voice coaches who usually directed their comments to me from across the room. When they told me to relax, to release my chin and open my throat, and to breathe more from my diaphragm, I was not in touch with my body in a way that allowed me to translate these excellent suggestions into the results that were desired. For me, there was a gap between receiving information of this type and knowing what to do with it.

Without hands-on instruction, it was very difficult for me to know if I had mastered a breathing technique or if my chin had released enough. Also, emotional issues would often close down my voice. I would use my loud sounds in a random way to open my throat, and my voice would be fine for an hour or two to do my broadcasting. But, because I hadn't psychologically worked through the issues that affected my throat, my voice would go back to where it was. As soon as I got another job, I would have to go through this all over again.

Later, with outstanding, supportive teachers like Ora Witte, Betty Cashman, and Eleanor Phelps, I did learn to enhance my vocal quality, but my self-doubts caused me to continue to feel insecure about my voice. Warming it up was always a hit-or-miss proposition and a source of tension whenever I had an audition.

In the midst of all my vocal turmoil, it sometimes amused me to reflect on the lengths to which other people would go to enhance their voices. Someone told me, for example, that the ancient Roman emperor Nero used to eat leeks to make his voice more sonorous, and the Greek actor Demosthenes used to put stones in his mouth. A well-known actress addressing an acting workshop I attended told the class that she couldn't give up cigarettes because she felt that smoking gave her voice its husky special quality that everyone liked. I heard that Lauren Bacall was directed to hike to the top of a hill and scream as loudly as she could as a way to deepen her voice. Carol Channing, it was said, out of concern for maintaining the arresting, raspy sound of her voice, once called in a throat doctor to be sure that she still had nodules on her vocal cords. So I was bombarded with all kinds of things people would do for their voices instead of some effective, reliable warm-up technique.

With less than full confidence in my voice, I never knew whether it would be there for me or not. I remember auditioning for one part when my voice remained low and full-sounding because I had a throat and chest cold. In fact, getting a cold—if I could miss the sore throat part—was great. It made me swallow a lot, lubricating my vocal cords; the tiredness distracted my mind and made me relax; and having moist, maybe inflamed, vocal cords lowered my tone a bit, giving my voice a deeper quality. So with the cold, I got the callback, but when I returned, the cold was gone, my voice sounded too high, and I lost the part. This lack of confidence in my voice was often discouraging, but I kept struggling. I thought, if I liked my voice when I had a cold, there must be a way to get that quality without the cold. I had a dream that I could have a wonderful voice. This was a flame that I kept alive, and I continued to persevere.

The Body Voice Discovery

The following years were rich with personal growth, artistic enterprise, career vicissitudes, and changes in geography as I moved in and out of the world of stage and screen and that of industrial communications. My career as a singer-actress brought me some exciting moments—a featured guest role on "The Honeymooners" TV show with Jackie Gleason and a principal part in a Florida revival of the musical *Call Me Madam* with Ethel Merman. Soon after these rewarding parts I went on to found and act as president of my own New York-based industrial communications company, Showcom. Then I returned to work in commercials and film, first in Washington, D.C., then later in the San Francisco Bay area, where I now make my home.

During this period, I also began the self-exploration that has been a constant part of my life ever since. I did private, group, and evening classes under the sensitive guidance of two brothers, Doctors Clinton and Clifton Kew to try to get some insight into the personal and emotional issues that affected my voice and my career—the emptiness that sometimes prevailed with both failure and success, in between my generally overly optimistic and enthusiastic zest for life. These rewarding hours laid the groundwork for much that was to come, but throughout all my career changes, I was still insecure about my voice and still warming it up by making random loud sounds and reciting poems at peak volume. Then, while I was doing voiceover and on-camera work in Washington, D.C., an event occurred that was to set me on the path to attaining the vocal solution I wanted.

One day, I was driving to the studio for three on-camera commercials and two radio spots for the Hecht Company, a major department store chain in the D.C. area. My voice was tighter and higher than usual and I was exhausted. I knew I had to do something to warm up my voice and get myself energized. I went through my usual warm-ups, but the minutes were ticking by and my throat was still tight. I began thinking that maybe this was my Waterloo, that all my years of hit-and-miss training were catching up with me and this time my voice was really going to let me down.

Groaning out of frustration, I clutched the steering wheel and shoved my left foot down on the floor. To my amazement, my groaning turned into wonderful sounds—big, rich, and deep. Hardly believing what had happened, I tried it again. This time, as I waited at a traffic light, I pressed both feet to the floorboard. As I pressed downward with my legs, my pelvis started to tilt forward, and I could feel the sound moving up through my body as I had never experienced it before. And my throat felt great. In fact, it was beginning to make sense that the more I pressed down with my legs, the more strength I was getting from my lower body, and the more my throat was able to open up and relax. By the time I reached the studio, not only did my voice sound just the way I wanted it to, but I felt more confident and energetic than I ever had after my usual warm-ups.

After this experience, I was excited. I thought, "So that's how I'll warm up my voice from now on. I'll make those deep 'huh' sounds and push my feet against the floor of the car all the way to the studio."

For some time to come, this was my method for warming up my voice. I used it with increasing comfort and effectiveness, but I still wasn't aware of the true importance of what I'd discovered.

Emotional Clues

It was in San Francisco. The director for a commercial I was voicing said to me, "My girlfriend is having a lot of trouble with the way she sounds. She's a beautiful model, and I wish you'd teach her how to have a lower voice."

I said, "What are you talking about? I've never considered myself a vocal coach."

He said, "Well, just show her what you do for your own voice."

This request took me by surprise. Yes, I did my own warm-ups, but I still considered my "huh" sounds, my speaking voice version of the "baby motor" drills I'd learned from singing lessons, and my leg pushing as my own personal thing. I certainly didn't think of myself as having voice techniques that might be helpful to others.

Nevertheless, I began to work with Tina, a stunning, tall brunette. The director was right: Tina was a real beauty, with poise and charm, and a face that became absolutely breathtaking on camera. But her voice sounded like she was still in high school. I showed her how to do my warm-ups, and she responded well, but it soon became obvious that a lot more was going on for her than simply releasing a deeper sound. While practicing the type of breathing I would later call Body Breathing, and attempting to exhale a full, deep sound, Tina told me that she experienced an inner resistance to letting go. She felt a need to hold on and fight the release. I soon found we were having some interesting discussions about emotions regarding her voice. She thought back over the vocal influences in her life, and remembered how her mother had repeatedly told her that she should be pretty as a picture, a doll who didn't talk. Each time she did my exercises, Tina found herself coming up against this secret injunction not to release her voice, but to keep quiet and be "pretty as a picture."

Once she was aware of this, Tina began to gently but actively work through this block, and her voice began to lose its little girl quality and deepen. I was glad for her, and amazed at the usefulness of my exercises. But most of all, I was fascinated by the implications of this experience. Here was a woman in her late twenties who, to judge by her appearance, was an accomplished adult. But to judge by the sound of her voice, she was an inhibited girl, unable to communicate fully who she had become. She had grown up in almost every way—except her voice. And this was because of the hidden yet powerful hold of her childhood vocal conditioning.

I thought back over my life and my vocal influences, searching for the kind of connections Tina and I had discovered about her early conditioning. I recalled a major humiliation I had suffered when I was nine years old and a member of our school's Brownie troop. We girls were playing some games before the meeting, while we waited for my mother, who was the troop leader. My mother had told me to tell the assistant Brownie leader she would be late, and I was filled with a sense of my own importance as the bearer of this message. The assistant was preoccupied directing the games, and I kept interrupting her to repeat my message. Finally, she lost patience and, turning on me, she yelled at me in front of the whole troop, "Will you please shut up? I heard you the first time."

Then, as a discipline or punishment, she made me sit out the rest of the game, humiliated in front of the others, for almost an hour until my mother finally arrived.

I remember how embarrassed and belittled I felt. My face

burned, my heart pounded, and my body shook. The hurt of her anger and verbal abuse went right through me. From that moment on, I was afraid of acting like a spoiled brat. The memory of it still makes me cringe. Her outburst made me think I was insensitive and unlikable.

Looking back now, as I had with Tina, I could see that after this traumatic incident, I had unconsciously developed two distinct voices. To follow my ambitions and excel, I adopted my father's authoritative, dynamic voice. With this strong, confident-sounding voice, I could be powerful in the world. When I used this voice, I felt I was emulating my father's sureness, and becoming an almost larger-than-life figure, the heroine of my ambitions and dreams. This was the voice I used as an actress and corporate businesswoman.

Whenever I had days filled with self-doubt, I tried to maintain this voice as a false front for my fears. Because waiting inside me was my other voice, a soft, timid voice, quiet as my mother's, ready to come out whenever I was vulnerable, shy, or afraid. I could see now why I had compensated by warming up my voice with big sounds. Whenever I approached a situation that caused me to feel afraid of rejection or failure, I would unconsciously start to use my mother's voice, timid and soft, afraid that if I acted too demanding no one would like me. It was clear that like Tina, some of my voice problems came from fighting my own inner emotional battles which then directly affected my voice. That day in the car, when I had pressed my feet to the floorboard and released deep natural sounds through a throat that had finally given up, I had apparently discovered part of the answer for solving my voice problems, for integrating my separate voice qualities and finding my own right personal sound.

Clues from the Body

Tina was only the first of many performers and professional people who came to me for help to improve their voices. Without fully realizing it, I began to develop the rudiments of a technique, a method that combined special breathing, body awareness, and the release of an individual, natural vocal sound along with exploration of the basic emotional issues in that person's life. As each person's story emerged, so did the connection to the release of a truly free voice. For one teenage girl, it was growing up in a large family where you had to shout to get any attention, resulting in a lifetime of expressing herself from an anxious, tension-filled throat. For another, it was a childhood of overbearing parents who repeatedly told her, "Don't open your mouth unless you can say something intelligent," resulting in a loss of spontaneity and a fear of sounding silly if every syllable were not planned in advance. For others, I touched upon much more serious, deep personal traumas and sometimes tragic backgrounds.

It was increasingly evident to me that the entire body was part of the voice. For example, in voiceover work, especially doing commercials, there are many styles of voice. There's what I call the real "Macho Crotcho" Voice for men doing hard-sell car and beer commercials. There's the Voice of God, the Voice of Authority, the Voice of Dad, and so on. For women, there's the Mommy Voice, the Granny Voice, the Pretty Voice, the Seductive Voice, and others. A whole constellation of vocal styles is used in radio and voiceover broadcasting to communicate types of personalities through the sound of the voice.

I would find that I could help people to reproduce voiceover styles most effectively by teaching them to put an entire body attitude behind each vocal character. For a Macho Crotcho commercial, the guy had to really let his whole body brag and boast. Or for a sexy commercial, you had to make your face, eyes, and voice sexy while letting your body take on a sensuous feeling. When doing a little girl, a wide-eyed face and innocent body stance added to the vocal believability. People may think of voiceover work as just using the voice, but that's a misconception, because it's acting the whole spectrum of the character—mind and body—to become the voice that communicates the whole story. And so, it makes further sense that to be yourself and to have a voice that effectively communicates *your* genuine personal qualities, you also must use your entire body.

It was obvious to me that my life was taking me in a new direction, and that I needed more growth and knowledge to pursue this path. It seemed I was becoming a combination voice coach and counsellor, so it was time to return to school to develop a firmer conceptual framework, gain more professional background, and, I hoped, come to a fuller understanding of the body techniques which seemed so powerful in helping people with their voices and emotional blocks.

I returned to school to pursue my Ph.D. in the field of body psychology while I pursued studies in many other facets of human behavior. In addition, I did my personal body, growth, and spiritual work with Dr. A. H. Almaas, who has developed what he calls the Diamond Approach for self-realization and who has been my primary self-development teacher. Gradually, I built up an understanding of anatomy and physiology to supplement what I was discovering about myself and the people I was helping. I delved as deeply as I could into the interrelation of voice, emotion, and body energy both in each person's vocal history and my own emotional development, as well as the refinement of my techniques of vocal improvement and expressiveness.

In my work with Dr. Almaas, I began to discover how my own vocal history was recorded in my own mind and body in ways I either had never looked at or had locked away at a very deep level. When I had been unable to produce the vocal quality I desired, I had usually passed it off as "just having a bad day." If I was very upset, I might go looking for a motherly hug from friends and an "It will be better tomorrow" philosophy—when all the time there was an underlying need to address my hidden tension and patterns of self-devaluation. Now, like another piece of the puzzle falling into place, I saw how my conflicts and fears over my voice were expressed in my body, and how my curiosity had led me to discover a voice-body-emotion unity.

I saw how my vocal problems had begun. As a child and teenager, I had had no idea how to simply let my voice be itself. Instead, I had a sense that I had to do something to it. My voice was far worse in my imagination than in reality. This was, I discovered, a period in my life when I was much too reliant on my intellect to solve every emotional issue. Like many of the people I now work with, I was living in my head, not in any kind of mind-body harmony. I remember that I was so much in my head that my emotional upsets tended to be repressed so that I wouldn't suffer. I would then think myself into feeling better.

For example, in my sophomore year of high school, my father died, and one of the ways my grief manifested itself was by disrupting my mathematical thinking. For almost an entire semester, I could not comprehend geometry. The world of triangles and axioms and proofs became a jumbled mess in my mind. Having been practically a straight A student up to this point, I suffered a lot from this blow to my record. It wasn't until the end of the semester that I started to recover from this mental block. Then, as time healed some of my grief, this aspect of my creative thinking returned. Geometry made sense once more, and I found I could prove theorems again, sometimes even finding interesting proofs the teacher hadn't considered.

Later, my emotional blocks moved directly into my throat. I remember distinctly that whenever I used to argue with my mother, I would feel my voice choking up. I internalized this tension completely, and all the time I was in school, I never knew when an attack of this kind would hit. Whenever it did, I would suddenly feel as if I were being strangled. I would gag and feel sharp pangs in my throat. By the time I was studying acting in college, there was a tight ball of tension in my stomach, and as my acting career progressed, this tension settled in my abdomen. During my early thespian pursuits in New York City, I drove myself hard, and feelings of pressure goaded me to do even more studying, more practicing, so I could get more acting work. I had my ambitions, and I was at war with my limitations. Fatigue, fevers, stomachaches—all were to be ignored, not acknowledged or succumbed to. The show must go on. I was driven as if someone stood behind me with a whip. Any time I thought of relaxing, I called myself bad, told myself I was doing less than my best, not giving it my all. It was only natural that my body would rebel with tension, which was reflected in my voice.

Eventually, I was able to heal the tension in my abdomen and release the energies I had held there for many years. Then I was able to open and fully relax my diaphragm, chest, and throat. And with this slow, somewhat painful, but always welcome recovery came a relaxation of my mental energies, a freeing of my thoughts from their tight, self-defeating limits. I was now able to integrate the vocal influences of my father and mother and those sometimes divisive parts of my personality. The result was a vocal quality that was my own fully personal sound, not bravely imitating my father to overcompensate for fear, and not held back with timidity to unconsciously attempt to please everyone the way my mother did. I found my own naturally powerful, expressive sound.

It took me five years to uncover what a full Body Sound was for my voice, but now I can help most people I work with get some experience of that sound in their first hour with me. By focusing on particular areas of their bodies and having them feel where the tension is, I can show them how to release a vocal sound that often surprises and encourages them about making their own BodyVoice discovery.

A Voice That Means Business

As I continued to learn about myself, my voiceover career was leading me yet again to new horizons. National Semiconductor Corporation had developed a talking electronic cash register, POS-italker, for countless grocery stores across the country, and they were searching for a low, warm, motherly, not-too-sexy quality in the voice they planned to digitize. When I was selected for this job, it struck me as ironic. My self-exploration and work with people's voices had become body-oriented, hands-on, and fully personalized, and yet I might be most remembered as the disembodied voice eternally chanting the prices of peas, popcorn, and paper towels in the grocery stores of the future. I also thought to myself that here was an interesting test of my BodyVoice concept. If my voice could retain even a portion of its alive, human quality when limited to a vocabulary consisting almost entirely of numbers—"two dollars and fifty cents; one dollar and twelve cents"—that would be split, mixed, rematched every which way and stored in a computer chip, then I would be satisfied. And indeed, supermarket surveys have shown that shoppers like the talking registers.

At the same time, I continued to work with many people on their voices. Eventually, I was drawn beyond the acting community. I began to work with politicians, service professionals, and corporate executives, At first, I was concerned with how my techniques and approaches would transfer over into the fact-oriented business world. John Naisbitt, in *Megatrends* and *Re-inventing the Corporation*, examines how people in high-tech environments look for "high-touch" experiences to humanize the impact of technology on their lives. Would this be true for business people concerned about their personal communication skills? Would corporate managers and entrepreneurs be responsive to my methodology and its inner process, body-oriented approach?

Tom, a corporate manager who had taken on the responsibility of leading a series of business seminars, was one of the first people I worked with in this arena. One of his friends had recommended him to me for some training in voice and personal communications. By the end of our initial interview, I knew that Tom would be a real test of my method. A handsome man with dark hair and serious eyes, he was as no-nonsense as they come. Tall, strong-jawed, straight-backed, meticulously groomed, he'd spent four and a half years in the Navy, most of it on duty aboard an aircraft carrier. After leaving the service, he'd entered and advanced steadily in the insurance business. He was divorced and had survived the dissolution of a fourteen-year marriage. Now he was adjusting to living on his own at thirty-eight.

Tom was someone who liked to take a hard look at who he was and how he dealt with the world. He was a problem solver who had his own tried-and-true ways of learning new things. When new experiences came his way, Tom had very set patterns for interpreting and understanding them. This doggedness had been a big part of his achievements. He had never been exposed to body-oriented psychology, and viewed the field somewhat skeptically. I explained to him some of the basics of my work with emotions and body energies that release the voice, and he freely admitted it was foreign to him. I often thought of him as my Doubting Thomas who would not believe until he could see for himself. But he was willing to try.

"I'll try anything that isn't dangerous or illegal," he said.

What Tom needed most was to learn to relax his body. From talking with him and observing the tense muscles in his neck and shoulders, I could tell that tension had a lot to do with the tight, restricted quality in his voice. He talked from the throat, because he lived there—in his head, neck, and shoulders—blocking himself off from tapping into his most powerful natural body energy sources. He was a self-driven person, and it was the anxiety and tension that drove him. He had a need to achieve, to reach out and master new areas, to push himself to be better and better.

Like I had once done, Tom was using his anxiety and tension as cues to controlling his behavior. A flicker of anxiety meant he wasn't working hard enough. Tension meant he was doing well, applying elbow grease, sweating honestly. A firm believer that nothing comes without hard work, Tom relied on feelings of tension and stress to reassure himself that he was giving it his best and not falling into a pattern of laziness or complacency. This strategy of self-orientation had been successful for Tom, but even he admitted that it left him with a nagging sense that he was missing something. Especially over the last two years since his divorce, he had found himself, despite continuing outward advancement, searching for a better sense of his own identity and some way to better ground himself in his life.

I suggested to Tom that what he was searching for was a

different kind of relationship with his body, one in which there was less tension and more responsiveness to his own spontaneity and feelings. Tom was skeptical, but we began.

For the first few weeks, I watched Tom go through a struggle common to people who are trying to switch from an overmentalized life to one of greater body awareness. Though I asked him to do exercises to focus his awareness on his arms and legs, and on his breathing, Tom's initial reaction was to send his mind racing through his body like a computer gathering data, then try to decisively analyze it, trying to reduce his sensory experiences to a success formula, which he would then report to me.

"Did I get it right?" he wanted to know. "Am I doing it right?"

"There's no right or wrong way to do it," I told him, to his consternation. "Whatever you experience is what you work with."

During this initial period, Tom's mind resisted his efforts to relax. What he experienced—body sensations, internal images, glimmers of sensory awareness—all seemed amorphous to him, nothing more than raw data gathering for his intellectual processes to understand and apply to improving the sound of his voice. He kept trying to treat his body like a jigsaw puzzle that he could put together to get the answer. He was used to analyzing problems and making quick assessments of feasibility and practicality. In every session with me, he was waiting for the solution to pop into his mind so that he knew he had it. And if not, he was geared to write off the experience as useless and go on to something else.

Then, in the fourth week, Tom told me that the process was beginning to make some kind of sense to him. We discussed this, and it turned out that what Tom meant was that he was beginning to *enjoy* it. Difficult as it was for him at first to change his perspective, Tom finally began experiencing his body as a source of energy and emotion. The stress reduction exercise I gave him now "made sense" because he could actually feel his tension draining out of his shoulders and neck as he focused his mind on the myriad sensations of weight, warmth, and aliveness in his arms and legs—sensations that were a pleasurable part of his individuality.

Of course, his mind was not ready to let go so easily. It still wanted to scan his body sensations with a robot's eye, identifying acceptable ones, discarding unacceptable ones. At this stage, Tom tried to categorize his different sensations as if he still believed I was trying to steer him toward a correct way to feel. Again, I simply told him that he should just experience whatever he felt and that there was no right or wrong way to feel during the discovery period. I just wanted him to be curious. Eventually, it started to sink in, and Tom was able to recognize that what he achieved by focusing on his sensations and letting them be was beginning to create a relationship with his body that was a way of feeling more aliveness and humanness in his daily life—the beginning of leading his life in a way that was kinder to his emotions and more relaxing for his body.

With this breakthrough, Tom progressed rapidly. He became better at letting his mind quiet down, and his body aliveness asserted itself more naturally. His jaw finally began to loosen from the grip of tension and his shoulders released. His breathing became fuller throughout the day, and he could feel the strength in his legs and all his inner sources of energy. Now, when he heard tapes of the seminars he was presenting, he no longer sounded too abstract or boring. Tom began to enjoy what he heard.

The final step for Tom was recognizing that he was starting to feel like a different person: himself. He experienced how he was feeling physically when he got his best ideas and had his most productive days. He began to enjoy his new relationships in a more sensitive way when he was in touch with his body. Soon this became his new way to interact on a daily basis, and the times when he had felt that it was normal to have his body geared up with tension and anxiety were gone for good. Looking back, he was shocked to realize just how much he had let stress be the main motivation in his life. Now, he found himself acting much more out of his own creative impulses. He was comfortable with himself and pleased with the quality of confidence and personal truth in his voice.

Four months after our work together was completed, Tom let me know that he was doing fine. His company seminars were getting great feedback, and all parts of his life, business and personal, were improved. From the confident sound of his voice on the phone, I felt sure that all these changes were lasting ones that he would reap many rewards from in the years to come.

After working with more people like Tom, I had no doubts that my method would be accepted by the corporate community and be a great asset to business people as well as performers. In fact, I have found my method to be helpful to everyone, no matter what their occupation or life-style.

Whatever it is that brings you to this book, my intention is to show you how to evaluate and improve your voice by looking at every facet of your communication impact. You may be confused about your voice. You may like your voice and just want to tune it up a bit. You may be afraid of public speaking. You may like your voice but get hoarse after long hours on the phone. You may not know what you sound like, good or bad, but have a feeling there's something off about your personal communication skills. To learn about your voice, you have to learn a lot of other things about yourself, and to do that, you have to look primarily at some important body considerations.

If you look at your voice without a body concept, you may get lost. You may run into obstacles and get unreliable results. I would like to think of this book as helping you find a solid way out of any misconceptions about how you come across in your personal communication. I would like it to help you discover *your* BodyVoice.

three

BodyVoice Evaluation

When Henry Higgins first raised an eyebrow at the sound of Eliza Doolittle's untrained voice, and began to consider her vocal potential, how did he go about evaluating her voice and patterns of communication? What things did he look for? What things did he feel it was most important to change? Are these kinds of things still valid today?

In the nineteenth century, when Victorian society idealized a straight-laced, stiffly mannered way of life and letter writing was still one of the most frequent means of personal communication, Henry Higgins relied on elocution methods. He wanted to improve Eliza's voice by teaching her to enunciate clearly, forming every syllable, emphasizing every consonant with precision. But today, in the era of global telephones and communication satellites, this style of speaking is no longer the fashion. In fact, when people learn to enunciate more naturally, they are able to release more sound and come across more believably.

Kevin, a professional historian who is often on the lecture circuit, came to me because he got some negative feedback from an audience, who found him too stiff. It wasn't his body or gestures, but that he enunciated every word as if he were trying to teach phonetics.

"But I thought I had to speak clearly for the microphone," he said.

"Not so clearly that it's an effort to listen to you," I replied. "There are other, more important qualities to work on if you want to be a dynamic communicator."

Today's winning vocal style is more natural, more personal, with the emphasis on a genuine quality of aliveness in the tone of the voice. You don't release this quality in your voice by enunciating in an elocutionary way. To speak with power and charisma, you need to develop your BodyVoice. You need to look beyond elocution, and become more knowledgeable about your body, breath, and emotions as they relate to your vocal characteristics. It is this kind of in-depth evaluation that can help you begin to improve the impact of your communication and discover your BodyVoice.

How You Perceive Your Voice

Evaluating your voice demands honesty and careful attention to both voice and body. You can get a better understanding of your voice by paying attention to several aspects of the BodyVoice concept. Specifically, you should consider carefully your own general *patterns of stress*. Your overall, conditioned ways of experiencing and coping with stress exert a powerful influence on your voice. Reducing stress appropriately is the essential first step in developing your BodyVoice. You should also consider your *body characteristics,* which reveal how in touch you are with your body energies. How you breathe and how comfortable and energetic your body is determine the aliveness, power, and personality of your voice. Your *vocal quality* is another important consideration. Most importantly, you want to evaluate the measure of aliveness in the sound of your voice. Finally, you should consider your *overall impact*. It will help you to have a sense of how effective your personal communication is, how close or far you are from having a BodyVoice style that communicates your natural personal charisma.

Begin with the BodyVoice Self-Evaluation questionnaire on pages 45–49 to understand these dimensions of your voice. Take five or ten minutes and fill out this questionnaire carefully. It can serve as a personal inventory of the physical, emotional, and vocal characteristics important to your communication skills. Note that the questionnaire consists of two types of questions:

Most sections are checklists of characteristics, symptoms, or situations. Check off all the items that are applicable to you. Feel free to check as many as you want. The number of items you identify does not indicate the full spectrum of vocal or communication problems you may have, but serves as a guide to some of the ways you may experience problems in public speaking, vocal expressiveness, or habitual tension. The more aware you are of how you communicate in a broad range of situations, the better.

The questionnaire also includes three scaled questions for you to give yourself a score of 1 to 10 on the status of your body characteristics, vocal quality, and overall impact. Don't feel that these scores are final assessments of your voice. As you will see, this is only the beginning.

As you fill out the questionnaire, you might wonder how you can be sure you are identifying all of the applicable items. How can you know what's appropriate? For example, under the Vocal Quality section, should you mark down that your voice has an unpleasantly high pitch if you're not sure how often this problem comes up? Perhaps it is only high-pitched occasionally, like the day you were nervous because a friend was tape recording you just for fun. If having your voice taped is not a regular part of your job or leisure activities, should you consider this a problem? To get the most useful results from the questionnaire, I recommend the following techniques to jog your memory and help you focus on what is really important to you:

Try to recall your feelings and behaviors in general throughout the course of a typical day, and then during periods of high stress and unusual circumstances. You may notice daily patterns; for instance, you might be aware of constant back tension or always being short of breath. Or you may identify specific reactions you may have to demanding situations, such as headaches when you have to work long hours, or getting concerned over your rapid heart beat when under severe pressure.

Think about the cycles and changes going on in your life—moves, career changes, new relationships. You may notice characteristics or problems that emerge during times of temporary crisis or as part of your personal evolution. You may notice that right now you seem to be in the midst of some kind of phase; perhaps you've been feeling tired the last few months.

Think about yourself in all sorts of places, at home and at work, and in all sorts of business and social situations, formal and informal. How do you talk, gesture, and feel when you're with friends, giving a speech, arguing, even thinking out loud?

You can take the BodyVoice Self-Evaluation questionnaire more than once. You can take it periodically—to keep track of improvements in your voice and communication style as you work with the Kenley Method. Or you can use it to create a profile of different phases or aspects of your life. For instance, you might want to fill it out for what you consider your normal day-to-day patterns of communication with family, friends, and associates, to examine yourself during those times you are not aware of any special demands on your voice. And then you might take it again for situations in which you are aware that how you sound is very important. Use a different color pen for your day-to-day responses and for your exceptional situation responses, and you'll be better able to pinpoint your specific problem areas.

For example, when Arthur first filled out the questionnaire, he identified the vocal stress situation in which he had the most trouble: giving a speech in front of a large audience. He also noted that talking with his family was often stressful for him, though he didn't see how it affected his voice. Nonetheless, to look more closely at the specific communication problems he had in each of these situations, he filled out the questionnaire twice again, once right after a company banquet during which he had to introduce the keynote speaker, and once after going out to dinner with his parents and other relatives to celebrate his aunt's birthday.

By recording his self-observations while they were still fresh, Arthur noted that at the podium he often had a choking feeling in his throat, sweaty palms, and a tendency to close his eyes, blocking out his audience. But at a family dinner, where he was continually engaged in one-to-one conversations, he discovered that he had the habit of constantly crossing and uncrossing his legs, as if he couldn't wait to leave the table. This discovery gave him a greater appreciation of how completely his body and his ability to communicate were affected by underlying tension. He was able then to look at his public speaking anxiety in the broader context of physical and emotional energy blocks, which helped him approach the enhancement of his vocal sound with much greater understanding than he'd had before.

Take your time with the questionnaire. Be honest and think seriously. This is an opportunity to start experiencing yourself and your life more fully. Enjoy learning what you know about yourself and your voice—and discovering what you *don't* know.

BodyVoice Self-Evaluation

This evaluation is in six parts relating to different aspects of how you experience yourself as you use your voice and speak to others.

Noticing Symptoms of Stress

Check off any of the following symptoms which may indicate personal stress patterns:

☐ Recurring headache
☐ Chest constricted
☐ Voice strained or hoarse
☐ Concentration impaired
☐ Tired and drained
☐ Faster heartbeat
☐ Shaking
☐ Stomach gets tight or upset
☐ Difficulty with breathing
☐ Sexual feelings diminished
☐ Lower back problems
☐ Other _____

Vocal Stress Situations

The following are situations which require interpersonal communication and about which you may feel stressed.

Circle the level of stress you associate with each situation:

	a. *Never*	**b.** *Sometimes*	**c.** *Always*
Interviews	a.	b.	c.
Giving a speech in front of a large audience	a.	b.	c.
One-to-one communication	a.	b.	c.
Speaking with someone in authority	a.	b.	c.
Talking in a small group	a.	b.	c.
Talking with strangers	a.	b.	c.
Talking with a group of friends	a.	b.	c.
Talking with your family	a.	b.	c.
Speaking spontaneously about something important	a.	b.	c.
Speaking on-camera	a.	b.	c.

Symptoms of Vocal Stress

Check off any of the following symptoms of stress you are aware of when speaking:

☐ Tight throat, choking feeling
☐ Sweaty palms
☐ Clenched jaw
☐ Headache, pressure around the eyes
☐ Spaced out or distracted feeling
☐ Butterflies in the stomach
☐ Shoulder tension
☐ Locked or shaky knees
☐ Shallow, rapid breathing
☐ Other _____

Body Characteristics

Check off any of the following characteristics that you are aware of:

Posture

☐ Rigid back and posture
☐ Depressed chest
☐ Legs seem awkward/nonsupportive
☐ Throat and neck seem tense
☐ Tendency to lean back
☐ Locked knees
☐ Face tense
☐ Drooping shoulders
☐ Lifted, tense shoulders
☐ Body seems disjointed
☐ Sagging posture
☐ Tendency to lean forward
☐ Good alignment/grounded
☐ Other _____

Awareness, Movements and Gestures

☐ Awkwardness or sense of discomfort in sitting, standing, walking
☐ Feel lack of body coordination
☐ Stiffness or hesitation in my gestures and behavior

☐ Sense of lifelessness in my physical expression
☐ Operating mentally, with minimal body awareness
☐ Sense of integration in my body and movements
☐ Internal sense of arms and legs
☐ Feel my sexual energy is part of my overall aliveness
☐ Ease and gracefulness in movements
☐ Aliveness and vitality in movements
☐ Other _____

Distracting Habits

☐ Lip sucking or licking the lips
☐ Clenching teeth
☐ Often shifting body positions
☐ Tensing eyebrows/forehead
☐ Hands around mouth while talking
☐ Scratching head
☐ Closing eyes/blinking
☐ Crossing legs
☐ Playing with hair
☐ Yawning
☐ Grimacing or making odd faces
☐ Distracting hand gestures
☐ Lack of consistent eye contact
☐ Nose breathing to talk
☐ Other _____

In general, I would say that my body makes me feel:
(Circle one number)

Uncomfortable	*Disappointed*	*OK*	*Comfortable*	*Alive/Confident*
1 2	3 4	5 6	7 8	9 10

Vocal Quality

Check off any of the following which seem to apply to your own voice:

Vocal Qualities

My voice:
☐ Tends to seem too loud for the situation
☐ Feels average and/or ordinary
☐ Has an unpleasantly high pitch

☐ Has a harsh, shrill or breaking quality
☐ Has a breathy quality
☐ Sounds too low
☐ Seems tight and under pressure
☐ Tends to be weak or inaudible
☐ Is appropriate to what is being expressed
☐ Sounds full and relaxed
☐ Is colorful and rich in texture
☐ Tends to be distinctive and alive
☐ Other _____

Vocal Style

My manner of speaking:
☐ Has a lack of articulation, a tendency to mumble
☐ Tends to be too fast to comfortably comprehend
☐ Is generally too slow
☐ Tends to include incomplete sentences
☐ Has exaggerated inflection or emotion
☐ Has a lifeless flat quality
☐ Is hesitant, with lots of pauses, or "ums"
☐ At times contradicts what I want to say
☐ Communicates what I feel
☐ Enhances what I want to communicate
☐ Seems to engage others
☐ Other _____

In general, I would say that my voice makes me feel:

(Circle one number)				
Uncomfortable	*Disappointed*	*OK*	*Good*	*Alive/Involved*
1 2 3	4 5 6	7	8	9 10

Overall Impact

Check off any of the following which seem to apply to you:

When I am communicating with people, I most often feel like someone who is:

☐ Insecure
☐ Scared
☐ Nervous
☐ Immature

□ Pressured and impatient
□ Angry or resentful
□ Hiding something
□ Unable to say what I mean
□ Arrogant
□ Weak
□ Detached and uncaring
□ Sad and lonely
□ Shy
□ Happy
□ Confident
□ Vital and dynamic
□ Easygoing
□ Authoritative
□ Responsive and sensitive
□ Thoughtful and caring
□ Truthful
□ Other _____

In general, I would say that my communication overall makes me feel:				
(Circle one number)				
Uncomfortable	*Disappointed*	*OK*	*Comfortable*	*Alive/Involved*
1 2	3 4	5 6	7 8	9 10

How Others Perceive Your Voice

Taking an honest inventory of your feelings, physical sensations, and self-perceptions is only the first step in evaluating your voice and the effectiveness of your personal communication. To know with some certainty how others perceive the sound of your voice and are affected by your communication, you are going to have to get feedback from those around you.

Taking this step can be one of the most rewarding experiences you can have. I can give you the following encouragement. There is probably nothing terrible about the sound of your voice. After working with thousands of people, I know that the most common negative perceptions about voices are that they lack color; that they don't effectively communicate; that they're ordinary, but not exceptional. This book can help you empower your voice.

The change in your voice that you need to make may not be

huge. Just six weeks of work on your vocal quality can lead to a much healthier, more vibrant voice. You know how when you're watching your weight, sometimes even two extra pounds can make the difference between feeling in top form or feeling uncomfortable. Once you become this sensitive to your voice, you will see how true this is of how you sound, and how even a small change can lead to greater confidence and empowerment.

Comparing your self-evaluation with other people's perceptions of you can help you become aware of precisely what you want to work on in your personal communication growth. After all, the essential feedback you want from other people is a sense of whether or not you are reaching them in the best way possible for you, helping you to evaluate the effectiveness of your communication.

To obtain precise feedback from others, use the BodyVoice Evaluation questionnaire. Make copies of pages 51–54 of this book, and ask five people you trust to fill out the questionnaire. They can do it while they're with you, or they can take it home and return it to you later. It shouldn't take them more than ten minutes to go through it. Try to choose a mix of business associates, relatives, and friends. Not all of these people need to know you well. What is more important is that they are caring, perceptive, interested in you, and that they will give you a sincere evaluation. Your associates may find that filling out the questionnaire is an educational experience for them, too. It can help them start thinking about their voices and how they are communicating.

Emily was a computer graphics artist and consultant who hesitated before taking this step. Finally, she approached five people: Sue, her best friend; Billy, her accountant and friend, whose perceptiveness and common sense had always impressed her; Margo, another graphic artrist whose low, musical voice Emily had always admired; Eric, an instructor at the computer school she had attended who had given her a recommendation, but hadn't seen her in some time; and Joseph, her current boyfriend.

To her surprise and relief, all of them were glad to fill out the questionnaire for her, and their evaluations, interpreted in the light of who was likely to be subjective, and who would be more objective, helped her target specific problems. For example, there was a spread on their ratings of her vocal quality, but everyone pointed out how tense her shoulders were. This was something she had not fully realized, and when she worked with me, she discovered how crucial it was to release this kind of tension to develop the personal sound of her voice. She was also surprised when Margo, despite her own attractive voice, expressed an interest in learning more about the BodyVoice concept. It seemed that though Margo was generally pleased with the richness of her voice, filling out the questionnaire for Emily had made her reappraise her overall impact.

"A lot of people tell me my voice is musical," she told Emily, "but I feel limited. It's not always appropriate to sound like I'm reflecting the same feeling. I realized that I want to develop a much broader range of emotional expressiveness."

Asking your friends to help you evaluate your voice can also be just their first involvement in your vocal changes. Friends and special others can help you at every stage of your development. They can tell if your jaw looks tense, or help you spot-check the sound of your voice. Friends won't know all there is to know about your exercises, but sometimes they may have a key piece of feedback that helps you along.

BodyVoice Evaluation Questionnaire

This evaluation is in three parts relating to different aspects of how this person presents himself or herself in the world. Each part has two sections:

1. Specific characteristics you may have observed in this person
2. A 10-point evaluation for you to gauge your overall response

The actual scoring is based on the latter question but the specifics can act as a resource for you to pinpoint your perceptions, as they will provide more specific feedback for the person requesting this evaluation.

Body Characteristics

Check off any of the following which seem to apply to this person:

Posture

☐ Rigid back and posture
☐ Depressed chest
☐ Legs seem awkward/nonsupportive
☐ Throat and neck seem tense
☐ Tendency to lean back

☐ Locked knees
☐ Face tense
☐ Drooping shoulders
☐ Lifted, tense shoulders
☐ Body seems disjointed
☐ Sagging posture
☐ Tendency to lean forward
☐ Good alignment/grounded
☐ Other _____

Movements and Gestures

☐ Awkwardness or sense of discomfort in sitting, standing, walking
☐ Lack of body coordination
☐ Stiffness or hesitation in gestures and behavior
☐ Body expression seems lifeless and/or mechanical
☐ Sense of integration about the person's movements
☐ Ease and gracefulness in movements
☐ Movements full of aliveness and vitality
☐ Other _____

Distracting Habits

☐ Lip sucking or licking the lips
☐ Clenching teeth
☐ Often shifting body positions
☐ Tensing eyebrows/forehead
☐ Hands around mouth while talking
☐ Laughing nervously
☐ Scratching head
☐ Closing eyes/blinking
☐ Crossing Legs
☐ Playing with hair
☐ Yawning
☐ Grimacing or making odd faces
☐ Distracting hand gestures
☐ Lack of consistent eye contact
☐ Nose breathing to talk
☐ Other _____

In general I would say that this person's body characteristics make me feel: (Circle one number)

Uncomfortable	Disinterested	OK	Comfortable	More Alive
1　　2	3　　4	5　　6	7　　8	9　　10

Vocal Quality

Check off any of the following which seem to apply to this person's voice:

Vocal Qualities

This person's voice:
- ☐ Tends to seem too loud for the situation
- ☐ Seems average and/or ordinary
- ☐ Has an unpleasantly high pitch
- ☐ Has a harsh, shrill or breaking quality
- ☐ Is appropriate to what is being expressed
- ☐ Has a breathy quality
- ☐ Sounds too low
- ☐ Seems tight and under pressure
- ☐ Tends to be weak or inaudible
- ☐ Is appropriate to what is being expressed
- ☐ Sounds full and relaxed
- ☐ Is colorful and rich in texture
- ☐ Tends to be distinctive and alive
- ☐ Other _____

Vocal Style

This person's manner of speaking:
- ☐ Has a lack of articulation, a tendency to mumble
- ☐ Tends to be too fast to comfortably comprehend
- ☐ Is generally too slow to keep me involved
- ☐ Is hesitant, with pauses, or "ums"
- ☐ Has exaggerated inflection or emotion
- ☐ Has a lifeless flat quality
- ☐ Tends to have incomplete sentences
- ☐ At times contradicts what is being said
- ☐ Seems to enhance what is being said
- ☐ Is dynamic and entertaining
- ☐ Keeps me engaged and interested
- ☐ Other _____

In general I would say that this person's voice makes me feel:
(Circle one number)

Uncomfortable		Disinterested		OK	Good		More Alive/Involved		
1	2	3	4	5	6	7	8	9	10

Overall Impact

Check off any of the following which seem to apply to this person:

When this person communicates with me, I most often get the impression of someone who is:

☐ Insecure
☐ Scared
☐ Nervous
☐ Immature
☐ Pressured and impatient
☐ Angry or resentful
☐ Hiding something
☐ Arrogant
☐ Weak
☐ Responsive and sensitive
☐ Detached and uncaring
☐ Sad and lonely
☐ Shy
☐ Happy
☐ Confident
☐ Vital and dynamic
☐ Easygoing
☐ Authoritative
☐ Thoughtful and caring
☐ Truthful
☐ Other _____

In general, I would say that this person's overall communication makes me feel: (Circle one number)

Uncomfortable		Disinterested		OK		Good		More Alive/Involved	
1	2	3	4	5	6	7	8	9	10

Scoring Your Questionnaires

Your BodyVoice Self-Evaluation questionnaire and the five BodyVoice Evaluation questionnaires filled out by your friends and associates are useful sources of information on your reactions to stress situations as well as vocal and body characteristics that you may want to improve as you work with the exercises in Part II of this book. As a convenient aid in assessing the overall quality of your communication style, look at the three 10-point scaled questions evaluating body characteristics, vocal quality, and overall impact on each questionnaire. Mark your scores on these questions from your BodyVoice Self-Evaluation and the five BodyVoice Evaluation questionnaires on the BodyVoice Evaluation chart that follows.

BodyVoice Evaluation Chart

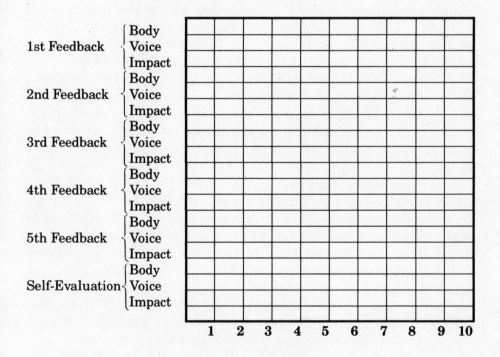

By noting where most of your scores fall on this chart, you can get an idea of how effective you are as a communicator.

If your scores are generally 9 or over, you are likely to be one who enjoys speaking and is inspiring to others.

With scores generally above 7, you are able to get your message across with a positive effect on others.

If your scores are generally 5 or below, then there are a number of specific skills and kinds of awareness you can work on to develop your BodyVoice and your communication skills.

If there is a large spread in your scores, it can be an important signal to you about some of the how's and why's of your communication style. Jonathan noticed that his friends and wife rated his voice and overall impact as much more expressive and effective than did his associates at work. This encouraged him to enter a period of career reevaluation in which he examined his life goals and much of the emotional tension surrounding his attitudes and decisions. This period culminated in his applying for and getting a much more satisfying position. A year later, he asked several new associates at work to fill out the BodyVoice Evaluation questionnaires for him, and he noted a big improvement in their perceptions of his vocal quality, as compared with his previous group of associates.

If you find that there is a large discrepancy between the scores on the BodyVoice Evaluation questionnaire and on your own self-evaluation, take an in-between score for your overall evaluation. Additionally, a voice coach or communication specialist can give you a professional analysis of your vocal qualities and communication skills.

Look back over the questionnaires, using them as an inventory, and you will be able to target some of your specific problem areas. Perhaps your nervousness in public speaking is a big factor in the way your voice comes across. You might notice, for example, that several people you asked to fill out the BodyVoice Evaluation questionnaire noticed you had distracting body gestures. This kind of inventory can be especially helpful to you when you begin to use the Kenley Method exercises and gain a deeper understanding of the effects of physical and emotional tension on your body and your vocal sound. The crossover relationships that occur among emotions, tense muscles, nervous habits, and your vocal quality will become more clear as you work with the relaxation, directed body awareness, and Body Breathing techniques and as you begin to experience the release of mind-body-emotion tensions.

For example, when I speak to a group, I have a simple way of demonstrating how unconscious or inappropriate gesturing can dramatically interfere with your message. As I demonstrate a mock presentation, I might show the effect of gesturing with irrelevant stabs at the air, or I might pace constantly, stand rigidly, or tap my foot. I might look around with wandering, unfocused eyes. The audience is quick to appreciate how distracting these various behaviors are. Then, when someone is working with me, I will explore how becoming aware of a distracting gesture can lead to a greater understanding of tension and the release of a full-body vocal sound.

Bernard, for instance, had the habit of stroking his chin and biting his lip whenever he spoke. Becoming aware of this habit led him to explore his doubts about his communication abilities, which in turn helped him resolve some of his fear of expressing his own thoughts and feelings to the important people in his life. He was able to develop a better understanding of how these nervous gestures impaired his potential to communicate with power and conviction.

As you use the questionnaires to understand the quality of your voice and communication, you may become aware of certain physical, emotional, or speaking problems that may benefit from professional attention. I encourage you to check these out before going any further. For instance, in evaluating your body characteristics, you might notice that your rib cage, neck, or back is extremely rigid or that your jaw is tense or locked. You might also notice problems with severe tension in your spine or symptoms such as grinding your teeth. In all such cases, it would be good to see your physician or chiropractor. If you have any problems with phonetics, a lisp, or a problem with your l's, a speech pathologist can be of invaluable assistance. Similarly, you should seek professional counseling for any emotional difficulties relating to how or why you developed certain common insecurities. Such support can be a powerful adjunct to using the exercises in this book. In fact, my techniques for vocal improvement are almost certain to help you find new ways of looking at yourself that will be useful.

Remember, though, that it is the emotional sound of your voice that makes it effective. There are many examples of people with some kinds of speech defects who have realized their aspirations. For instance, Barbara Walters and Tom Brokaw have certain speech idiosyncracies that get characterized and sometimes satirized, but they are still highly successful on-camera journalists. What can hold you back is a dull voice lacking in aliveness, and a style of communicating that doesn't reflect your inner vitality.

Evaluating Your Communication Proficiency

When you begin to use the Kenley Method exercises, you will be learning to reduce stress and to increase your breathing power and speaking charisma. It can be helpful to you now to evaluate your communication in terms of your proficiency in each of these three areas. The Kenley Method Proficiency Guide, on the following pages, describes three levels of proficiency for each area:

> Level I indicates problems in awareness and communication skills with the resulting lack of BodyVoice power.

> Level II indicates improvement, greater understanding, and effectiveness.

> Level III is that of a person who has mastered the Kenley Method techniques and has become a dynamic, powerful communicator.

Read each section of the Proficiency Guide carefully and decide how each item applies to your voice and communication. Then check the appropriate level for each dimension of your communication on the Proficiency Self-Evaluation chart on page 61.

The Kenley Method Proficiency Guide

BodyVoice Stress Reduction

Level I

- Your lack of awareness of tension buildup, physically and vocally, causes you to suffer from symptoms of stress: headaches, gut in turmoil, constricted chest, tight stomach, breathing difficulties, vocal strain, diminished sexual aliveness, and loss of concentration.
- You operate in a mental mode, cut off from bodily sensations.
- You can be perceived as scared, intimidated, nervous, and lacking in credibility because your body is awkward, your voice is unsure, and your gestures mechanical.

Level II

- You can identify where you chronically harbor tension buildup in your body.
- You have learned specific techniques to control and dissipate your tension.
- You begin to notice your voice and body are experiencing fewer debilitating symptoms of stress.
- You might be perceived as generally competent with a measure of believability.
- Your physical and vocal expression do not detract from what you are saying.

Level III

- You demonstrate the ability to cope with ease in tension-filled circumstances.
- You can detect and manage stress before it becomes detrimental.
- You are perceived as relaxed, confident, engaging, and full of vitality.

Body Breathing Power

Level I

- You have never considered how you breathe or how breathing affects your vitality and your health.
- If your breathing is deficient, you could suffer from lack of energy, respiratory difficulties, diminished sexuality, depression.
- You could be perceived as weak, inexpressive, lackluster, or powerless.

Level II

- You know how to breathe using your entire torso.
- You begin to experience the pleasure of more energy in your daily life.
- You are gaining a sense of solidness and well-being.
- You may be perceived as somewhat energetic with a measure of initiative.
- You have a certain personal presence and strength.

Level III

- You now Body Breathe naturally.
- You are using the power of your lower body to support your breath.
- You experience a calm sense of personal power.
- Your gestures and body movements have an attractive fluidity.
- You are perceived as energetic and confident, with a powerful personal presence.

Body Speaking Charisma

Level I

- Your speaking voice lacks color, resonance, and power.
- Your voice has no connection to your legs and lower torso, your sexual energy, or your life energy.
- You have no personal connection with your message or your audience.
- You are perceived as too mental, having phony energy, more interested in content than contact, vocally ordinary or deficient.

Level II

- You notice when you are throat speaking or Body Speaking.
- You see how your vocal qualities dramatically affect others and their perception of you.
- You are beginning to give more support to your voice from your lower body.
- You will be perceived as communicating in an integrated way, with an interesting voice and an expressive body.

Level III

- You are Body Speaking with an alive, exciting vocal charisma.
- You dynamically communicate a personal sense of who you are with your body and your voice.
- You are perceived as a persuasive, energetically alive person with charisma—one who speaks in a rich and vibrant way.

The Kenley Method Proficiency Self-Evaluation Chart

Check your perceived level for each category of proficiency to get an overview of your current communication impact.

Level	Stress Reduction	Breathing Power	Speaking Charisma
I			
II			
III			

You can use this guide to evaluate yourself now and at any point during your work with the exercises. Update your Proficiency Self-Evaluation chart as necessary to measure your progress.

Don't be hard on yourself. Grow at your own pace. Honor your own personal value and keep going. Enjoy the progress you make.

Don't compare yourself to others or to an arbitrary standard. Compete with your own skill level, not with others.

The Kenley Method Proficiency Guide can become a permanent part of your life, serving as a framework for keeping in touch with yourself and your best energies. A few years ago, I went to Spain on business, and after a day of conferences, I agreed to have dinner with Leah, an interpreter for the American embassy. Leah had worked with me the year before to improve her vocal quality so that she could be more effective as a translator. She had gone on to many achievements in her field, culminating in her position with the Embassy. As she drove us into town, I was surprised when she put on an audio cassette and suddenly I was hearing my own voice:

"Hello, Leah. Today we're working on producing Body Sounds."

"That's the tape I made for you!" I exclaimed.

"Si, Señora," she smiled. "I listen to it every morning when I'm in the car."

I was delighted she was still listening to the tape every day, reviewing the steps of the Kenley Method, going through her vocal warm-up. And I was very moved to observe how she had grown through using the tape during the past months.

"And I use your Proficiency Guide, too," she said. "I've looked at it so many times, I've got it memorized. What do you think? Am I on Level II or III today?"

I remembered what Leah had been like when we first met: a stickler for accuracy, often frustrated by the vagueness of the language. At one point, she had even thought of abandoning her dreams, despite her bilingual abilities, because she thought she didn't have the temperament for it. She'd filled out the BodyVoice Self-Evaluation questionnaire and noted right away all the arrows pointing to her tense mental efforts: concentration impaired; headache, pressure around the eyes; tensing eyebrows/forehead; operating mentally, with minimal body awareness. Discovering and learning to trust in her body energies had been the key for Leah to draw on her inner resources and abilities.

Now, driving down a winding road in Marbella, I gave Leah a quick evaluation. I looked at the way she held herself, this handsome forty-five-year-old woman, her air of relaxed confidence and competence. Her face was alert and glowing, and her voice had a quality of pleasing, serious strength—just the kind of voice you could tune in to amid the hubbub of an overlapping simultaneous translation. When I considered her overall impact, I felt the presence of a delightful, thoughtful communicator. Her style and impact were certainly inspiring.

"Well?" Leah laughed, waiting for my reply.

I smiled back. "Level III all the way," I said.

I hope you have a sense now of how you can use the tools in this chapter to evaluate your personal communication. To sum up, I recommend the following steps:

Create a folder for your BodyVoice Self-Evaluation questionnaire, BodyVoice Evaluation questionnaires, BodyVoice Evaluation chart, and Kenley Method Proficiency Guide, or use whatever means is most convenient for you to keep these where you can retrieve them for easy reference.

Fill out the questionnaires in three-month intervals to measure changes in your voice and communication and to check your progress.

Refer to the BodyVoice Self-Evaluation questionnaire as frequently as is effective for you to pinpoint problem areas and troublesome situations.

Periodically, ask friends and associates to fill out the BodyVoice Evaluation questionnaire for you. Especially when you've changed circumstances, or find yourself with new acquaintances or partners, you may learn much.

Use the Kenley Method Proficiency Guide to evaluate your voice and your communication impact as you progress.

Remember that your voice is a part of a BodyVoice unity, and by periodically evaluating your personal communication impact and vocal quality, you are also keeping in touch with your personal energies, and that is an important part of your health, success, and well-being.

four
De-Stressing

It's been a stressful day for everyone. Sometimes you can just tell; it's something almost palpable you can feel in the air. The evening rush hour traffic is worse than ever, and the business news of the day makes it clear that life is getting tougher. You can see the tense faces in every car that goes by. You can hear the strain in the harsh sounds of people's voices, at the gas stations, in line at the automatic teller machines, on your own answering-machine when you replay your messages. When you talk to your friends, you're almost afraid to ask, "And what kind of day did *you* have?"

I'm sure you've had days like this. Everyone seems to be taking his tension home with him. What do people do to relax and get that tension out of their systems? Almost every evening I see a neighbor of mine out jogging. She's in her shorts and Reeboks, with her Walkman on, heading for the bikepath that runs along the beach. She always has such a look of punishment on her face that I can't help wondering if she's really pleased with the way she's managing herself after a demanding day. Many times I've ended my work day at a business meeting, and I hear people making their plans to unwind. "It's been a long one," says a friend, "and I'm going to pour myself a strong one." I know his favorite lounge. It is a cozy, comfortable place, but I again wonder if a few drinks and an hour of relaxed bar conversation will be sufficient to take the knots out of his shoulder muscles.

"There's only one way to get these kinks out," says another man, winking after a long stretch. We laugh because we know what he means. He was telling us earlier that his wife just flew back into town after a big out-of-state convention, and he's looking forward to the night. I know this is a common perception, that sex is a great tension reliever, but looking at how stiff this man's neck is, I can't help but think, "Doesn't he have a way to not get so tied up in the first place?"

Managing stress and tension is essential for your health and your enjoyment of life. It is also crucial to developing an effective speaking voice and becoming a dynamic communicator. Let us now address the *causes* of stress in your life, not just what temporarily treats the symptoms. Too many people try to reduce stress by flagellating their bodies into submission, rather than by discovering a comfortable energetic ebb and flow. Managing tension should mean more than just an aerobics class twice a week or occasional down-time in front of the TV, more than taking a ski trip or soaking in a hot tub. It should be something you do throughout the day as part of a natural cycle of action and relaxation to prevent the kind of build-up of tension that can be so destructive to your physical well-being and vocal expressiveness. Consider:

> Stress and tension powerfully affect your body, your voice, and all aspects of your personal communication.

> Habitual patterns of stress—how you routinely express or hide emotions—can become chronic states of body tension which dramatically inhibit your vocal aliveness.

> It's not simply reducing your level of stress, but experiencing the innate self-esteem of your stress-free body, that gives your BodyVoice its personality, power, and charisma.

Stress Hide and Seek

For most of us, it's not too difficult to begin to identify some of the superficial sources of stress in our lives. No doubt you can pinpoint right away many of the tension-producing elements in your daily activities: managing your finances, dealing with competition and personality clashes at work, balancing relationships, scheduling car repairs and dentist appointments, and trying to keep it all straight. Sometimes there are specific situations that seem to bring out your worst. Perhaps the BodyVoice Self-Evaluation questionnaire helped you identify some of these stressful times when you have the most trouble with tension and your voice. But digging deeper, it is often difficult to find the ingrained patterns of living and reacting to life's demands that cause a great deal of the hidden stress in your life. You might be able to put a finger on a few obviously traumatic events—a divorce, the death of a loved one, a move to a new city—but the deeper patterns of stress and their causes are often harder to identify.

Enjoying the expressiveness of your BodyVoice and becoming an effective personal communicator involves your entire mental, physical, and emotional presence. You need to listen to your body, learn to hear what it is saying, and understand how to be guided by physical sensations. However, most of us start out with a well-established pattern of defending ourselves against our awareness of physical sensations. In fact, most people live in varying states of physical contraction to ward off feelings of chronic pain or unwanted emotions. These contractions anesthetize the capacity to experience personal interactions in your life in a complete way.

By the time you are an adult, the process of blocking out certain reactions becomes so efficient that trying to stay in touch with pleasurable feelings and body sensations is like playing hide-and-seek and finding no one: you simply cannot contact the energies that would be able to flow through your body without these chronic physical inhibitors. Often, you don't even realize the negative state of your body. Before you can release a contraction, you have to become aware that you have one. For example, you might not even realize how constricted your throat is until you feel it begin to loosen up. In fact, for some people, relaxation can initially awaken body sensations of discomfort or soreness, as more life energy flows into the chronically bound places that have been numb for so long. This numbness begins in childhood from contracting various parts of the body to avoid vulnerability, pain, anxiety, crying or fear.

This need for *control*—control of feelings, behavior, and life circumstances—is often expressed by tension and tightness in the front of the throat and neck. Similarly, fear often resides in contracted muscles in the back of the neck. So, if you are a person who is both afraid and has a need for control, you may literally feel strangled when trying to handle these emotions, because you've put a psychophysical vise around your throat.[1]

---

[1] Ron Kurtz and Hector Prestera, *The Body Reveals* (New York: Harper and Row, 1976), pp. 68–69.

When your jaw is tense, your throat constricted, your lips tight, or your shoulders rigid, any or all of these symptoms can appear in your voice. Your voice may sound hard, controlled, or harsh. Do you really want to have a "stiff upper lip" or to "keep your chin up"? Do you really want to "swallow" your rage or your tears, or "take it in the neck"? It can be very difficult to let go of that kind of tension if you feel it's the very thing that's supporting you and holding you together. Your body, however, needs a relaxed, confident flexibility to produce a rich, powerful voice.

What about you? Are you holding emotions in? Are you tense without even realizing it? Here's a simple way to check for tension in your neck. Very gently put your fingers on both sides of your neck while you are speaking, and see if your muscles are rigid or actively moving. What you should feel when you are talking correctly is a soft, vibrating skin and neck tissue, with hardly any action in your neck muscles. If your neck muscles feel hard and tight, then you are probably harboring some inhibiting tension.

Stress Ups and Downs, Ins and Outs

There are many ways in which your body can try to handle habitual stress and tension, none of which are particularly good for your health or your voice. In some people, stress tends to elicit the kind of emotional arousal that causes the "fight or flight" reaction, with its characteristic rapid heartbeat and faster breathing. You may have experienced this state when your car started to skid on a rain-slick road or when a customer suddenly withheld his signature from a vital contract. You may also know someone whom you would describe as generally "overcharged," "hyper," or "all jazzed up," someone who seems to find almost all demanding situations stressful and tries to cope with everything in an overstimulated state. This person eats fast, talks fast, has thoughts racing a mile a minute, and has every half-hour planned with frenetic activity. All this nervous activity gives a superficial impression of energy and aliveness, but it soon becomes apparent that underneath, the muscles are tensed and locked up. It is easy to lose yourself in the Bermuda Triangle of tension formed by your head, neck, and shoulders. A block at this level effectively cuts off your mind and your voice from the rest of you. Tension in your neck and throat is like a log jam that blocks the healthy fluidity of your body.

When you're in a constantly overcharged state, you're literally off in your own head, cut off from a constructive perspective on your nervousness. If you're caught in a traffic jam or late for an appointment, you're as tense as if you're in the jungle, where any moment a tiger might pounce on you from a nearby tree. This kind of inappropriate nervous arousal is a waste of your vitality. It's like using an industrial power plant to heat your home. It robs you of health and well-being, and diminishes your capacity to communicate. In fact, I've observed that overcharged people often do not hear well; their attention is elsewhere. Truly they cannot enjoy or benefit from the full capabilities of their own bodies and senses.

Another reaction that affects some voices is the kind that elicits the body's sleep and relaxation responses, with its characteristic slower heartbeat and breathing. If you've experienced this state when you want or need to be more energized, you know what it's like to feel you're moving in slow motion, with no thoughts and no desire to do anything more demanding that watching TV or listening to the radio. You feel undercharged, undervitalized. You don't have the resources for a powerful voice.

People living in an overcharged or undercharged state often have sexual problems. In general, any energy deficiency will cause a decrease in sexual interest or capability. States of overstimulation or lack of energy can occur for biochemical as well as emotional reasons. For instance, hormonal imbalances related to the adrenal and thyroid glands can strongly affect how energetic you feel and how your voice sounds.

Your goal should be a flexible balance between states of arousal and relaxation. A constant state of battle readiness will not serve you as well as the ability to be relaxed when necessary, alert when necessary. Just picture a cat curled up on its favorite cushion, totally relaxed, grooming itself or resting in the sunshine. But the split second there's the sound of barking nearby, the cat is wide awake, muscles ready to pounce or bolt. As soon as it's clear that no dog is going to come bounding into the room, the cat returns to its relaxed repose almost instantly. Unfortunately, people rarely use their energy with such healthy economy.

You learn your own way of maintaining an emotional balance as you go through life, but external success is no indication that you have even addressed an effective way to deal with stress. Whatever level you're on—secretary, housewife, company president—you have some tension button that sets you off and starts habitual responses in your body, a surge of hyperactivity, a tensing up, a withdrawal, or numbed-out avoidance. You will tend to carry your tension baggage with you—often right on your back—as you move up the ladder. And as pressure increases, so does the effect of all that tension and your body's ways of coping with it—and so does the effect of all that tension on your voice.

Think for a moment about the kinds of situations, the types of people, the places and occasions, even the gestures, facial expressions, and vocal qualities that frequently seem to trigger your tension. What gets to you? Is it fighting to get information out of someone who won't give you a straight answer? Is it bending over backwards to please everyone at a family holiday dinner? Or rushing to make an early morning meeting on time? Is there a certain sarcastic inflection in someone's voice that fills you with hurt and anger? Do you have a general feel for how your body charges up, or goes numb? How your mind suddenly zooms in or spaces out? What about your voice? Does it rise in pitch, or sink into a weak, hoarse whisper? Do you notice any patterns of tension or vocal inhibition that seem to have been with you for as long as you can remember? You may discover more than one long-established pattern, because many of your habitual ways of coping with the kinds of stress that affect your voice are learned in your early life experiences.

Your Vocal History

Your personal behavior and coping strategies have their roots in your innate nature, parenting, and environment. So, too, how you communicate and interact as an adult—and what qualities your voice has—is related to your early heritage. Taking a look at the early years of your life from a BodyVoice perspective can give you a sense of the story of your voice—what vocal qualities you started with, what influences affected your voice, and most importantly, what stressful and even traumatic experiences have become entangled in your personal communication style. All these elements are part of your vocal history, and knowing that history can be a great help in understanding the current behavioral patterns in your life that affect the sound of your voice and your personal power.

Like everyone else, you started out in life with distinct and individualized vocal abilities. Your parents probably remember all too well your first vocalization: crying. You'll remember we discussed a typical day in the life of your adult voice, showing you how different the vocal qualities are that you use to communicate with your business associates, friends, and lovers. Your specific way of vocalizing your messages began when you were a newborn, when you had several distinct types of crying, each of which effectively communicated your needs and desires to your parents. Like all babies, you had a Distress Cry; you wailed, and your mother or father came running. Your parents were also probably quite used to responding to your Hunger Cry. Some lactating mothers find this rhythmic scream so effective that a burst of this type of crying is sufficient to release their flow of milk. You no doubt also had an Angry Cry that made it clear when you were unhappy, and an Attention Cry to demand play and kisses and hugs from your parents.[2]

Stress, and its effect on your voice, is also present from Day One—and even before. If a mother has a high-risk pregnancy or difficult delivery, it is more likely that her baby will have higher pitched, more piercing or grating cries than babies from low-risk pregnancies.[3] These differences can be clearly perceived by adults.

An infant's crying is soon supplemented by cooing and then babbling. At this stage in your vocal history, you were not only expressing yourself, but learning to take on some of the intonational patterns of adult speech. Even at six months, you were creating a pattern of playful communication with your parents. You exchanged smiles and cooing and other sounds in a manner highly responsive to the adult playing with you. Your entire infant body was involved in this play—the way you moved your head and used your eyes, wiggled your fingers and toes, turned your hands and feet, twisted your little torso. And of course, you used your voice, in imitation of and response to the adult making funny, probably high-pitched baby talk to you.[4] In fact, you pattern how to move your tongue, jaw, throat, and chest from this imitation, and take on the breathing and speaking mannerisms of your parent, whether or not these patterns

[2] Edward Tronick and Lauren Adamson, *Babies as People, New Findings on Our Social Beginnings* (New York: 1980), Collier Books, pp. 109–125.

[3] P. S. Zesking and B. M. Lester, "Acoustic Features and Auditory Perceptions of the Cries of Newborns with Prenatal and Perinatal Complications," *Child Development*, 49 (1978), pp. 1155–1162.

[4] Tronick and Adamson, *Babies as People*, pp. 126–150.

are natural to you or fit your innate personality. This stage of communication very possibly also had its stressful side. If your parent was not responsive to you, your first relationship was probably painful and taught you to physically withdraw feeling and energy from your body and voice.

One of your parents' treasured memories is probably the day you spoke your first word. But once you learned to express yourself with language, your vocal expression may have been shaped and inhibited by confusing messages from your parents and other adults about your behavior and, especially, about your voice. Much of the tension adults have often originates in habitual reactions learned during this stage of childhood. Many children have parents who tell them to "Stop crying." If yours did, you probably responded by holding in your breath, eyes, face, mouth, and throat to cut off the sound and the emotion. Other children are constantly admonished, "Be seen and not heard." If this happened to you, you couldn't let out your vocal and emotional communication of anger or joy. These types of experiences are so common that the sound of the voice is one dimension that psychologists have been able to use to detect differences between children's ability to trust and go out into the world. Young children who tend to be inhibited in their responses to unfamiliar people and situations frequently have a voice pattern indicating greater tension in the vocal cords than do more uninhibited children.[5] Once these vocal patterns are learned, they remain with you until you find a way to unlearn them.

Children at this stage of development are acutely sensitive to criticism and to the way that emotions are expressed in their families. Whether your parents and teachers told you that you were bright or stupid, attractive or ugly, appreciated or just a nuisance, had a powerful effect on your self-esteem, your way of relating to your body, and on the developing quality of your voice. Your parents inevitably expressed themselves to you and to each other in characteristic ways. Each had his or her Relationship Voices for interacting with each other—for being close, for fighting, for managing problems. In some families, the norm is yelling, carrying on, singing, and arguing. In others, it's politeness, not complaining, and smoothing over conflicts. As a child, you perceived and unconsciously imitated these vocal characteristics which now give your adult voice some of its special qualities of expressiveness and dialect. But those

---

[5] Research by Jerome Kagan, reproted in *Psychology Today* (April 1984), p. 68.

same characteristics can also be a source of undesirable vocal qualities.

I remember an incident with Lois, a truly talented investment counselor, and a working single mother as well, who came to me for help with a dull, hesitating, stuttering voice. We worked until she felt comfortable with the fluid sound of her BodyVoice and the Body Speaking techniques which had eliminated her speaking problems. One day, I called her home to confirm the time of an appointment, and her ten-year-old daughter Cathy answered the phone. Cathy's voice sounded like her mother's had when I first met her, only younger. It had all the lifeless hesitancy that her mother's voice had had before working with me. Later, I asked Lois if she had ever noticed this similarity. She hadn't. After our discussion, she'd talked to Cathy about their voices. To her surprise, her daughter had said:

"Oh, you mean I should talk like *this*?"—immediately letting her voice relax into an imitation of her mother's fuller, confident sound.

Here was a clear demonstration both of how a child learns vocal qualities from parents, and of the flexibility of youth. A voice *can* change with an educated ear and with the correct influences. The incident also made me reflect on why Lois hadn't picked up on Cathy's vocal characteristics until I pointed them out to her. I realized that in daily life with its many demands, people don't seem to pay much attention to the familiar vocal cues or patterns of close family members or long-term partners.

To investigate your own vocal history, you might ask yourself these questions about your childhood:

Was I told to be seen and not heard?

Was I often reprimanded and told to "shut up"?

Did my parents shout or were they quiet?

Did I frequently yell, or was I the silent type?

Was I acknowledged as clever or told I was stupid?

Did I grow up in a nurturing or a negative atmosphere?

Does my speaking voice sound like either parent?

Was my upbringing emotionally free or restricted?

Was my sensual aliveness encouraged or ignored?

Answers to these questions can help you discover many of the habitual pathways by which stressful situations affect your body and trigger inhibiting responses that are reflected in the sound of your voice.

The Attacking Voice

As you trace your vocal history, you are likely to discover that one of the most powerful stress factors in your life is your self-monitoring mental chatter—an internalized sense of self-disapproval that continuously observes, judges, and belittles your every thought, feeling, perception, and effort. This part of you attacks you for imagined failings and shortcomings. It's an inner, silent Attacking Voice in your mind that usurps the flow of what could be your healthy BodyVoice, that inhibits your true vocal expressiveness and devitalizes your body energies.

You might want to stop for a moment and reflect on the ways your own Attacking Voice speaks to you. If you keep a journal of this daily mental commentary, you'll find it relates to Should's, Ought To's, Might Have's, Wish I Were's, and Why Can't I's. It can be constant or intermittent, distracting or subtle. It can skip from subject to subject without apparent logic or doggedly return to the same thoughts time and time again. Experts in the study of human dynamics have long pointed out how much energy can be tied up and wasted in this kind of mental activity. The Eastern meditation traditions sometimes characterize this aspect of the mind as an untamed wild ox or unstoppable wild elephant trampling your mental clarity, or as drunken monkeys making a chaos of your focus and decision-making abilities. It is well-known that stressful situations increase this kind of chatter until your mind is filled with so much noise you can't think straight.

Frequently, however, your Attacking Voice is not content to merely confuse you and trip you up. At times it can be much more damaging. At its worst, it is a persistent tormentor, which actively interferes with your life and causes great suffering. Some common self-criticizing scripts are:

"I wish I looked more professional."
"I came across as ineffective."
"I should have done it better."
"I ought to be able to get it perfect."
"Why can't I be the best?"

Also, you can become obsessed with what other people are thinking about you, how they perceive you and judge you:

"Do they respect me?"
"What are they thinking about me?"
"Did they think I was in their league?"

Or you may lose your sense of solid accomplishment in worrisome, grandiose self-appraisal:

"I'm the only one here who knows what he's doing."
"I don't need to listen to other people."
"I can do it all by myself."

Some of you may not think on first self-inspection that you have an Attacking Voice. However, if you feel generally lethargic or withdrawn, you may be refusing to listen to an implied attack. If you have a chance to come out of your state of emotional shutdown, it's likely you'll start to feel the guilt, worry, and other reactions related to a self-attack. Soon you'll be able to identify the types of thoughts that oppress you, whether or not they are clearly verbalized in your mind.

Different schools of psychological theory have given various names to the Attacking Voice—the Superego, the Critical Voice, the Judging Parent—but all theorists are in agreement that you can't develop a relaxed, self-confident identity as long as your own mind victimizes you. If you cringe before your own negative thoughts, or if they mislead you with a false sense of accomplishment, you can't function from a place of objective reality. If your Attacking Voice has you at its mercy while you're trying to succeed in your business, then the important facts you want to recall, the clients you want to be attentive to, and all other important details can just disappear from your grasp. You're often at a disadvantage when you feel nagged or distracted by negative mental chatter, or when you are physically suffering from your body's stressful reaction to the attacks. Your throat can be a primary target, and you may find your words literally getting caught in your throat as your vocal cords fill with tension.

Unfortunately, the Attacking Voice is common in our modern society. Too many of us have to some degree learned to internalize a need for high performance and achievement, and to interpret setbacks not as lessons and challenges, but as failures. Many people have also, to some degree, learned to cope with this sense of failure by criticizing themselves harshly for every imagined character fault that might be the reason for failing to perform at high, or even unreasonable, standards. I have demonstrated this fact to groups by asking each participant at a communication seminar:

"How did you attack yourself this morning on the way to the seminar?"

The room resounds with the laughter of recognition as each person trots out the favorite ploys of their Attacking Voice that are familiar to all:

"I didn't prepare enough."

"I should have gotten more sleep last night."

"I'm not smart enough to understand the things I'm going to be asked to do."

"Everyone in the workshop will think everything I say sounds uninteresting."

People are always surprised—and relieved—that other people also suffer from these self-putdowns. Many presume, "Everyone's got their act together but me." You, too, may find it liberating to realize that you are not alone, and that your self-criticisms are probably overly harsh, not kind, and often inaccurate.

Take a moment and try this exercise yourself. What important activity was on your agenda today? What does your Attacking Voice have to say to you about it? Take a look at these attacks, and realize that everyone around you has their own Attacking Voice probing for the holes in their self-esteem with the same or similar thoughts. You can learn to quiet your Attacking Voice with the process I will share with you later in this chapter.

Managing Your Tension

The negative effects of stress and tension provide a familiar litany of ills to be avoided. Physical tension interferes with mental clarity and creativity, has destructive effects on your heart, blood pressure, and other internal body functions, and even seems to weaken your immune system. The combined effects of stress can strangle your voice and inhibit your vocal expressiveness, plunge you into a pattern of frantic activity or plummet you into lethargy or withdrawal. The Attacking Voice can drive you into lifelong patterns of procrastination, anxiety, and inaction. Constant nervous arousal can make you feel that you are always in danger, as though threatened by a fire-breathing dragon, even when the threat is only in your mind, or involves a problem that you would realize you are perfectly capable of solving—if only you weren't undermined by tension.

What can be done?

The first and most important step is to recognize that tension is in fact something to be managed. Too many people, despite all the popular attention to stress management, still think of tension as unavoidable. They still believe that the price of a fast-paced lifestyle is losing the relaxed, natural enjoyment of their bodies into what I've described as the Bermuda Triangle of tension.

Jack was an articulate young man who at first strongly resisted the idea that tension buildups could be prevented. Thin, wiry, with dark, witty eyes, Jack was a fascinating person. He was bright and had an instinct for current cultural and business trends. He had all the makings of a great journalist or social commentator.

"I've always wanted to know everything I could about what's going on around me," he told me on our first interview. "I subscribe to twenty magazines—and read them all. And I ask all the people I meet what they think about the world, because I think everyone has some insight, some privileged viewpoint. I'm really curious, and really concerned."

With his dedication, quick mind, and sensitivity, he was certainly deserving of success without paying the high price of tension. Like many people, however, he came to me with a voice problem that would lead him to reappraise many aspects of his personal style.

Jack had used his talent and determination to became staff writer for a prestigious feature magazine and had learned to adapt to constant deadlines. But every time he had to hash things out with his editor and boss, his voice choked up. When I pointed out to him that some of the tightness in his voice was caused by the constant tension in his head, neck, and shoulders, Jack was quick to let me see that he already knew all about it.

"That's where my tension goes," he said. "Every time. When I have a deadline, I glue myself to my chair and work with total concentration. Usually I've got a hundred and ten loose pieces of information flying around that I have to organize and synthesize into a coherent article. I don't have time to relax."

After years of hard work and self-discipline, Jack felt that he knew himself and his habits, his strengths and weaknesses, his physical and emotional limits. When he was caught in a crunch, and had no choice but to put in long hours at his desk, pounding away at his computer, raiding vending machines for late-night pick-me-uppers, he could feel the tension of the deadline going right into the muscles of his neck, his shoulder blades, and the back of his skull.

"I just loosen my tie and collar, and go at it," he said. "I can feel my shoulder blades rising and coming together, and my head sinking down into my shoulders, until I feel like a vulture hunched up on a branch over a highway, waiting for a tasty morsel. Believe me, I know every cramp, ache, and twinge in my neck and back, and exactly when to expect them. That's just part of the job."

In fact, Jack almost boasted of his ability to take the punishment, to absorb and endure this tension. At least he knew if he took minibreaks and rested his eyes occasionally, he wouldn't get headaches. But as for the buildup of tension deep in his muscles, that permanent sense of blockage and stiffness, the diminishing mental clarity as he pushed himself on and on, he felt there was nothing to be done.

"It becomes a part of your mindset," he told me. "Every deadline, every crunch, reminds me of previous ones and takes me back to the first time I stood in an editor's office, sweating like mad, and wondering how on earth I was going to do three weeks of work in one night. Of course, that was before I found out I had superstamina. I've never missed a deadline."

"But," I asked, "what if you could learn that relaxing can improve your efficiency and not at all diminish your capacity?"

Jack thought about this, then smiled. "I guess my image of myself at work is like a character in a spy novel, the kind of guy who's got the weight of the world on his shoulders. The kind of guy whose life consists of Styrofoam coffee cups and long sleepless vigils in smoke-filled rooms sifting through tapes for the secret message, who gets awakened every morning at 3 A.M. by a phone call about someone getting murdered. I wouldn't feel right if I didn't wake up with bags under my eyes. That's just the way you get work done in my business. You pour it on. When you've met your deadline, then you can unwind. There are times when you just have to ignore your body."

"Jack, that's not such a wise idea," I had to say. "When tension builds up, it's not just your body that gets lost. It's *you*—who you are, what you are, what you could be."

A look of concern and dissatisfaction crossed his face.

"It's too bad," he said, "that loosening your throat isn't as easy as loosening your tie."

He was thinking, he told me later, of what he was like when he went in to face his editor. Then he didn't feel like a man with superstamina, or like a master secret agent—just a person under pressure whose voice sounded throttled.

I have found that the most effective way to reduce the harmful effects of stress and tension that affect your voice is a combination of relaxation, Body Breathing, and body focusing that I call the De-Stresser Technique. The key is to draw your attention toward the emotionally neutral territory of your arms and legs, away from the body battleground of emotional and physical turmoil in your mind, throat, chest, or gut. By Body Breathing and holding your breath in a particular way, you can restore balance to your body and mind when they have lost their normal, healthy pattern of charging and discharging tension. As we've seen, no one needs to be tense constantly, as if always ready to escape possible danger. When there's no need for action, you want to enjoy a sense of quiet aliveness. This means allowing your body to discharge its energy effectively, not just by trying to relax at the end of a long day, but by dealing with tension at its source. When you've learned to release tension as soon as is necessary for your body to regain its equilibrium—by using relaxation techniques, Body Breathing, and body awareness continually as a natural part of your daily activities—you can *prevent* chronic muscular contraction, mental noise, and states of agitation or lethargy.

When you use the De-Stresser Technique and start releasing your tension, you can find the strength and confidence and relaxation that come naturally to you when you're in touch with your body. Part of the technique is letting yourself feel any sensations that occur—as long as you focus your awareness on sensing your body. You might experience a state of deep relaxation, like the kind associated with yoga and meditation. You might have a sense of healing wounds as you work through emotional pains from your past. Or you may experience nothing more dramatic than an indescribable, unmistakable sense of your own personal body quietness. There's no right or wrong way to feel—only your way. It doesn't matter whether your body has a rich sensory vocabulary or a strong silent flow. The important thing is to release the ravages of tension and enjoy the deliciousness of your body's stress-free state. This enjoyment of your body's aliveness, whether orchestral or quiet, is your cue that you're reemerging from your habitual tension and on the way toward releasing the potential of your BodyVoice.

Quieting Your Attacking Voice

When you begin to relax and become aware of your body's aliveness, you've also taken a first step toward quieting your Attacking Voice. This is because destructive mental chatter comes from a tension-filled mind, and it gets even more free reign when your body is tense and contracted. By releasing tension using the De-Stresser Technique, you free many of your feelings and emotions. As we will work out together, the more you become tension-free, the more you free the energies of your heart, lower body, and sexual aliveness. These freed-up energies are powerful sources of self-esteem and make your Attacking Voice seem ridiculous and misguided. It's hard to let an attack such as, "I should have done better," get to your throat when you can feel vitality and aliveness in your body and your voice.

The key to success in coping with stress is a quick recovery time from distressing episodes. That is, an ability to accept that you are going through a tension buildup and to take appropriate action on the spot.[6] This is why I developed the De-Stresser Technique as a portable exercise that you can use before a meeting, on a plane, in a reception area, on stage before stepping up to the podium, or anywhere you need it to calm down before going into action.

It will be extremely helpful for you to have powerful techniques at your command for mastering your Attacking Voice in quiet moments or in times of high pressure. I recommend a specific set of tools for dealing with the Attacking Voice. This is a process, developed from seminars with my associates in my psychological work, which can help you respond rapidly to an attack from your inner critic and disengage your mind and body from the stressful effects of the attack. You can learn not to accept the attack, not to consent to

[6] Jerry Giles, *Psychological Immortality* (New York: Richard Marek Publishers, 1981), p. 181.

the insinuation that you are a bad or less-than-perfect person. You don't need to punish yourself by letting all that tension soak permanently into your body.

The process of quieting your Attacking Voice was a great help to Jack, the staff writer who seemed so attached to his patterns of absorbing and retaining muscular tension. Showing how he learned to use it will demonstrate how the technique works. Jack needed it most the day after he'd put in all-nighters, when his editor wanted his final reports. Jack knew that pacing his work was a big challenge, and despite his professionalism in meeting deadlines, there were always factors beyond his control. He was always dependent on information from other staffers which might be late and cause him delays. Even after years of experience, he still dreaded that moment in his editor's office when his boss would glare at him and demand, "Well, are we going to put this one to bed on time?"

As this inevitable confrontation approached, Jack's Attacking Voice went on a binge of recriminations.

"I didn't work fast enough last night," he'd tell himself. "I shouldn't have stopped for dinner. I should have been twice as far along as I am." By the time Jack stepped guiltily into his editor's office, his nervous system was shot, and his voice was stifled and defensive.

As I worked with Jack to develop his speaking voice, I also helped him learn how to use seven steps to quiet his Attacking Voice. Over the course of several weeks, here's how Jack ultimately learned to disengage from self-attacks as he approached his editor's office.

1. Recognize the Attack

The first thing Jack did was to be conscious that his Attacking Voice was on a rampage. As soon as he realized that he was thinking, "I should have worked harder last night," he made a mental note that an attack was beginning and he got ready to cope with it.

2. See/Feel the Effect of the Attack

Jack learned to be very aware of the tension building up in his body and he soon knew the effects to expect from the attack. Particularly, he knew that his throat often felt like a vise and his voice lost all its power.

3. Identify How the Attacking Voice Wants You to Feel

Jack's Attacking Voice wanted him to feel like a bad child with a guilty conscience. It wanted him to feel that he deserved to be abandoned to his Bermuda Triangle of tension, that he should drive himself harder, and punish himself for any desire to attend to his other emotional needs. Jack could feel a sense of shame for not behaving like a flawless, unflagging machine. How dare he feel justified in confronting his editor as an equal when he had brought in his own verdict on himself as deficient?

4. Determine How This Feeling Negates Who You Are

Jack found this step particularly helpful. Even if in the heat of the moment he was not able to deal with his Attacking Voice's message or see it as untrue, he could see clearly how the Attacking Voice's apparent purpose was destructive, not helpful, not on his side. Realizing that, right or wrong, the Attacking Voice was hurting him always brought Jack a sense of indignation. He would note to himself, "This is not constructive criticism of a possible mistake I've made. This is pure intimidation, outrageous and out of line."

5. Mobilize Energy to Disengage

Here the De-Stresser Technique was invaluable for Jack. No matter where he was, even walking down the corridor to his editor's desk amid the hectic rush of the office, he could take a few moments to concentrate on his arms and legs as he walked, notice the flow of his muscles, the feel of his feet in their shoes, the notepad gripped in his fingers, the in and out of his breath. The De-Stresser Technique broke up the building tension. Sometimes, he would also take a few quick deep breaths and stretches to help energize his body.

6. Select an Appropriate Method of Disengaging

Once Jack had followed the above steps, he found that his body felt alive and that his Attacking Voice was not the overpowering ogre it had seemed. Now he was able to take it on with any number of mental attitudes based on a better sense of self-esteem. The following table illustrates some of the methods you can use to quiet your Attacking Voice. Jack found that sometimes surrender was a particularly effective method. He would respond to an attack, "Go on. I know you're never satisfied." Other times, humor was effective: "You're right. It's obvious I didn't work hard enough—I'm not hospitalized." Jack learned that these comebacks to his Attacking Voice came naturally and spontaneously once his emotions were released. They were what he naturally felt, how his self-esteem would respond under any undeserved attack.

Methods of Quieting Your Attacking Voice

Indignation	Let your sense of anger and dignity swell. "I don't deserve to be treated this way."
Truth	Rest on your common sense. Your Attacking Voice is never logical; it always overgeneralizes, takes things out of context, and conveniently forgets mitigating circumstances. Just tell it, "That doesn't make any sense."
Humor	Wittiness is a great way to defuse a situation and confuse an attack. "I only let bullies say that to me."
Exposing the Judger	Your Attacking Voice is a great one for not being able to take what it dishes out. "Who are you to judge?"
Exaggeration	Taking the attack to an extreme can expose its absurdity. "Yes, I'm the dumbest person in the country."
Agreement	Opposition kindles resistance. Why waste energy fighting yourself? "Sure, whatever you say."
Indifference	You're a busy person. Your Attacking Voice must prove to you it's got something meaningful to say before you'll listen. "So what? Who cares?"
Surrender	Giving in to your Attacking Voice can put it on the spot. Suddenly, its big accusations look like petty quibbles. "Go ahead, do your worst."
Active Visualization	Imagine some action that halts the attack. Pack those accusations into a rocket, shoot them into space, and explode them.

7. Verify Your Effectiveness in Disengaging by Checking Your Body's Response

Jack learned that it was easy to tell when he had won. A peaceful confidence returned to his body, and he entered his editor's office energized and ready to negotiate for what he needed to meet the deadline. His throat was relaxed, and when he spoke, it was with the confident flow and natural authority of his BodyVoice.

Quieting your Attacking Voice can become like second nature to you. Once you've learned to recognize and disengage from self-diminishing attacks, you'll have a welcome sense of relief—"OK, I know how to handle this"—and you'll no longer be victimized. Also, logically enough, the same techniques can be used to vocally defend yourself when someone else tries to disparage your efforts or humiliate you. Intimidation by others often works by triggering the same self-defeating emotional and physical reactions of guilt and unworthiness. Learn to stop needling yourself, and you'll have learned a lot about maintaining your self-esteem when you have a confrontation on your hands. By disengaging from the internal attacks that inhibit your voice, you'll be able to summon more of your natural vocal power when you need to stand up for yourself.

Finding Your Personal Power

No discussion on stress can be complete without looking at the stress that arises from changing your personal life-style. This is especially true when you are developing your BodyVoice. The choice to change your vocal quality can feel risky. It's easy to fall into the familiar stress patterns—either hyper and overcharged about changing, or skeptical and doubtful, trying to convince yourself that the change is not worth the trouble. Changing the way you sound may make you apprehensive about the effect your new BodyVoice will have on the important people in your life.

Cheryl, whose girlish voice was an expression of a generally timid personality, asked, "Will my boyfriend object now that I feel and sound stronger? Will my mother?" Leonard, a gruff product line manager who felt that barking orders was what won him respect, was afraid that if he released the hardness in his voice and enhanced the richness, he would seem less masculine. Peter, a corporate executive in danger of becoming a workaholic, had so much of his identity wrapped up in tension and resistance to feeling that he was afraid if he changed his usual way of functioning he'd have no power left. He was sure he'd lose control and be overwhelmed.

Developing your BodyVoice can be much easier if you use the following Process of Understanding, a guideline for working on

yourself in a healthy, nonjudgmental way. With the proper attitudes, the stress of change need not overwhelm you. The following
five-step process can be useful for embracing any type of learning
experiences or changes in your life.

Process of Understanding

Awareness. Begin by developing an objective understanding
of how your body and emotions are intimately connected with the
potential expressiveness and power of your voice. You can become
more aware of yourself as an individual with a unique set of stress
patterns and vocal qualities. You can learn about your own vocal
history and set your own course for releasing hidden tensions,
contacting specific body energies, and discovering your innately
expressive BodyVoice.

Curiosity. Observe the changes in your vocal quality in a
spirit of active investigation of your true nature and your potential.
As you overcome blocks and inhibited speaking habits, you will
make exciting discoveries. You'll discover that you are able to extend
yourself and your capabilities in ways you didn't think possible.
When you start paying attention to your body and your voice, you'll
find you begin to notice the bodies and voices of other people in a
more perceptive way. Your whole life can have more color as you
notice the constant fluctuations and exchanges of personal energy
that make up human communication. Be open to new experiences
and enjoy the new, more personal way you will sound and interact
with other people.

Compassion. Don't lose sight of compassion—kindness for
yourself and others—as you grow and gain in personal power. So
many of us lack compassionate attitudes toward ourselves in our
careers and personal lives. I hear constantly from people, "I hate my
voice. I hate my hair. I hate my clothes." Self-hate eats up your
energy and makes it difficult to appreciate anyone else. The more
loving you can be to yourself and the more forgiving about your own
foibles and failures, the more generous you can be with other people.
Compassion for yourself will make changing your voice all that
much more possible.

Courage.   Why do people let their hearts harden, their lower torsos become insensitive, their sensuality shut down? Often the reason is that living in your own mind seems much safer emotionally. It takes courage to break those old barriers and to begin living more fully. It sometimes also takes courage to face the important people in your life who may be disconcerted at the changes in you as you develop your BodyVoice. As we will see, a woman whose voice is small and childish may sometimes feel she doesn't have the strength to stand up for herself. Cheryl discovered that the men and others in her life who were used to her accommodating behavior had to adjust to her BodyVoice and her new assertiveness. Some of her friends came to terms with her as a person who looks, acts, and sounds like an adult. With other people close to her, she had to redefine relationships.

Patience.   Let the process of change work on you and in you at its own pace. Don't let your Attacking Voice get a hold on you because you think you're not progressing rapidly enough. After working with hundreds of people, I can assure you that you will progress and you will discover and develop your BodyVoice—and in less time than you might think. An attitude of patience helps you relax and stay open to the experience of your body aliveness. Be aware, curious, compassionate, and take heart; you will find your BodyVoice and understand how it can enrich so many aspects of your life.

five

From Body Breathing to Body Speaking

They'd read it in a magazine, that the fear they suffered from was rated by Americans as their Number One fear, worse than fear of flying, worse than fear of any disease. And they had it: the fear of public speaking.

Her name was Julie. His name was Frank. They were corporate team members in a technical training department who had come to me for help with improving their presentations at the training courses they gave to their company's clients. Julie was a tall brunette with clear, keen brown eyes and straight, shiny, classically styled hair. Frank was broad-shouldered, fair-haired, and wore designer glasses that gave his light-colored eyes a powerful, penetrating look, which combined with a broad smile gave him a seeming air of command.

I observed both of them carefully. I noticed that Julie had a few unconscious habits that distracted me when she spoke. First were overlong pauses which, instead of giving her words greater emphasis, actually confused her intended message. Also, while she paused, Julie's eyes wandered, looking at everything except me. And despite her generally smart appearance, her posture betrayed a lack of vitality. We were sitting for this introductory interview in my office. Instinctively, Julie had seated herself in one of the big cozy chairs and was slightly slumped in a way that seemed more in retreat than at ease.

Frank, on the other hand, sitting in a straight-backed chair, seemed very alert, almost too alert. He had a way of rigidly drawing himself up, holding in his stomach when he talked, so that despite his energetic air, he appeared uncomfortable, as if he were pinned together somehow and if one pin were to pop, he would deflate like a balloon.

I listened carefully to their voices, too. Julie's voice gave me an impression of someone lacking strength or passion. Frank's voice had a nice hint of fullness to it, but it came out sounding cramped, with a hard edge, despite his genial smile. He spoke rapidly, getting out long sentences without pausing for a breath. He seemed to become self-absorbed in midthought and forget there was someone he was trying to communicate with.

"Tell me about your jobs," I said.

"We work for a manufacturer of word processing systems, a big company with a lot of small-company entrepreneurial spirit, where we're supposed to enjoy doing a bit of everything," Frank's words ran on and on. "We do programming, design review, sales, instruction."

"Instructing, yes. That's where the problem began," interrupted Julie. "When a company buys one of our systems, we install it and send an instructor on-site for two weeks. We rotate instructors. And this year, it's our turn to go on the road."

"Sounds like it should be fun," I said.

"Oh, it could be," she said. "I like traveling and meeting new people. But when it's time to give the course and stand up in front of twenty people, well, I just feel myself turn to jelly."

"I get some of the same feelings," said Frank, jumping in. "But not every time. I think it has to do with how important or new the contract is. If I know a big purchase is at stake, I worry about it while I'm talking, and I can't stay in touch with where I am or what I'm saying."

"With me," Julie mused, "It's the number of people. Five, ten, even fifteen seem okay to me. But more than that, and I feel like I'm up against walls of eyes closing in on me."

"Then, too," Frank confessed, "some of the people we have to instruct know so damn much. They've worked with every system on the market. Suddenly, there you are, with all these stony faces, all looking skeptically at our course materials, daring you to prove to them that your system will not be a big headache."

"I know," said Julie. "And it's not that I'm unprepared or don't know my stuff. I bring extensive outlines and notes with me. And I know every nuance of our software."

It was clear that Julie's fear of speaking before groups had nothing to do with lack of competence. Also, her problem was not a lack of vocal potential. As she spoke with me, her voice momentarily escaped its prison in her throat and swelled with enthusiasm for her work, and her sense of her own personal power poured out. Her speaking problem was a deeply conditioned fear that arose in stressful situations, eroded her energy and confidence, and robbed her of that beautiful voice whose potential I was hearing now.

But then, something interesting and revealing happened. As Julie noticed me reacting positively to her, taking in the energy she had momentarily beamed my way, she suddenly became self-conscious, paled as if she'd done something wrong, and visibly shrank. I watched her catch her breath and hold in her stomach. I noticed this, because I was paying special attention to the way she breathed.

The characteristics of your breathing patterns—the sound, rhythm, volume, speed, and muscular movements of the chest and abdomen—can tell a great deal about your emotional and physical state. As you learn to become more aware of your breathing, you can start to observe the meaning of different ways of breathing in yourself and in the people around you. For example, if you talk extremely rapidly, you're probably not in touch with your body, but more in your head. If you talk too slowly, it might be fear of saying the wrong thing, or you might have a dry mouth, which is a common effect of nervousness, as is its opposite, producing too much saliva. Observing your breathing can also give you a sense of how comfortable you are with your body. High, shallow breathing commonly indicates tension. A serene facial facade coupled with fast breathing can indicate a dichotomy in your emotions.

Frank meanwhile was shaking his head.

"We've got to do something to be more effective instructors," he said. "The kinds of questions the class asks sometimes make me realize I'm not communicating as clearly as I could."

"Is it any better in one-on-one situations?" I asked.

Julie and Frank looked at each other as if, in their search for an answer, they had discussed this between themselves.

"Sometimes," said Julie. "If I feel the other person is sympathetic and I can stay technical. But if it's a confrontation or argument,I have a lot of the same discomfort."

"Me, too," said Frank. "I just seem to check out. I go off into limbo."

"I go rigid," Julie added. "Or I can sense my body behaving weirdly, my hands pointing randomly, my knees shaking."

"And my voice," Frank frowned, "sounds like it's coming out of a nearby loudspeaker, not from me at all."

Both of them looked very distraught now.

"What about your breathing?" I asked.

"Oh, I tried that," said Julie. "I was told that I should breathe deeply from my diaphragm. So, I practiced deep chest breathing until I thought I was pretty good at it. But the first time I had to give one of my courses, I felt the panic. So I did my deep diaphragmatic breathing. It didn't help. I was still upset. My head felt light and my stomach felt like a fish flopping out of water."

"I've felt like that," said Frank. "One time I felt faint and had to interrupt the course for a few minutes while I sat down and got my equilibrium back."

Julie nodded, then hesitated before going on. "I also found something disturbing. The deep breathing made me feel worse sometimes. I had a sense of . . . well, I don't know why, but often I suddenly felt sad and I wanted to cry."

She looked at me as if she expected I'd tell her she was crazy.

When I just nodded with understanding, she continued. "So, I stopped using the deep breathing. In fact, I found that keeping my breathing as shallow as possible gives me at least some control. I go into my training courses holding myself together by a thread. But it makes me feel bad. I feel shut off, like I'm hiding from myself. But I just don't know what to do."

"I think I can help," I said. "First, both of you need to work on your breathing in a way that *can* overcome many of your problems—Body Breathing. You'll discover what it has to do with your fear of public speaking, your lack of body aliveness, and your sense of strong emotions lurking just under the surface."

The Many Tasks of Breathing

I'll return to Julie's and Frank's story in a moment and show how they worked through the facets of their fear of public speaking. But first, I want to discuss why, especially if you're like Julie or Frank, it's essential to look at how you breathe and to understand Body Breathing. Like most activities of the human body, breathing performs more than one crucial function and is an integrated, inseparable part of the healthy functioning of other body systems.

How you breathe can help manage your body's reaction to stress. Specific ways of breathing can help energize you when you need to go into action, or calm you down when you need to relax, as well as recover your energy after a taxing episode. Managing tension, and experiencing your stress-free body, is essential for releasing the power and confidence of your BodyVoice.

Breathing performs another vital function in your life. As is well-known, it is the exhalation of breath through the vocal cords that produces the sounds used for speaking. Also, the way that the breath is inhaled and released is directly related to the strength, tone, and quality of your voice. Your breath can be like a column of air supporting your voice, and how you breathe can either give your voice the foundation it needs or undermine it.

Your breathing patterns can also be associated with your body posture and your muscular tension, as well as your ability to feel and express your emotions. Your adopted pattern of breathing is another key to understanding the relationship between emotional and physical tension in your life. To feel fully alive and in touch with your body's energies also requires what I call Body Breathing.

Why Body Breathe?

Body Breathing is the most natural, effective way you can breathe. It is a way of breathing that brings optimal benefits to your body and your voice. Body Breathing means using a breathing movement that involves your entire body, especially your lower torso, not just your diaphragm and chest.

Many voice teachers tell their pupils to focus their breathing on the movement of the diaphragm located at the bottom of the rib cage. But if you're emotionally and physically kayoed by the idea of giving a speech or telling someone how you really feel about something, what set of muscles in your body usually collapses first? For many, the area of the diaphragm is what usually takes the emotional blow. If you're stressed or fearful, it can feel like the middle of your body's caved in, or like you've been socked in your stomach. You're probably familiar with this sensation—"Oh no, I locked the keys in the car!" "What do you mean the report's due today?" "Who was taken to the hospital? Is it serious?"—like a boxer's glove going straight to your midsection. If that's where your breathing is centered, then when you get tense, your breath has nowhere to go but up. Your breathing gets caught in your chest and throat, and your voice can get shaky or smothered. Your body may literally retreat, shutting off your feelings. You may begin gesturing awkwardly, struggling for words.

However, if you Body Breathe, centering your breathing movement in the group of muscles you cough with in your lower torso, you can bring the aliveness of your pelvis and the strength of your thighs and lower legs, plus the strong muscles of your buttocks, to the active support of your voice. If you face an audience and feel slugged in your solar plexus, you can keep your balance, emotionally and physically, by calling on the support of your lower body. Relying on these large muscles for your support, you can more easily allow your throat, chest, and stomach to relax. Body Breathing is like putting the furnace in the basement of the house where it belongs. The heat can rise up from below and warm the whole house. Your breathing can come up through your entire body and support your voice. You can speak from an energized mind-body, without anxiety and nervousness cutting you in half.

This type of breathing is part of your birthright. Healthy babies and animals Body Breathe naturally without having to learn how. But as you grow up, the way you breathe can change without your being aware of it. Your breathing patterns as an adult are not innate, but picked up from the breathing patterns of your parents and other role models. The way you learned to breathe is part of your vocal history. You learned your posture and the way you hold your chest and abdomen muscles from your home life and culture. You even arranged your neck, throat, and jaw muscles to talk the way your parents and others talked.

Think back for a while and ask yourself, "When I was growing up, how did my parents breathe?" Try to remember how they spoke. Were they fast talkers, or slow talkers? How did they hold their backs and their shoulders? How did they tilt their heads? I can remember some of my parents' breathing patterns. My mother would sigh a lot, a characteristic kind of sigh, exhaled from the middle of her body. My father was a fairly deep breather. A good way to jog your memory is to think about your childhood suppers or holiday dinners. Table talk is an especially rich occasion for observing how your family members interact, talk, and characteristically breathe.

All too frequently, what you may discover about your childhood is the restricted breathing movement you developed. But try to imagine what a baby's breathing is like. A healthy baby breathes fully, its whole body gently moves, unobstructed. A baby's emotions are also unobstructed. Feeling is huge in a baby's body, because an infant has no way to monitor, defend against, or dilute its bodily reactions. When parents give approval or disapproval for an infant's experiences of pleasure or pain, a baby learns not to yell too loudly to express happiness, not to cry too much to show distress. And the most effective way for a baby to control emotions and body sensations is to hold its breath—to constrict the muscles used in breathing, especially the diaphragm. This breaks the wholeness of the breathing movement, and obstructs the experience of natural emotions. Thus, the baby loses some of its natural aliveness and the full enjoyment of its body.

Holding your breath may still be part of your way of coping with strong emotions, just as it was for Julie when she first came to see me. Even animals do it to cope with danger. When a deer hears a threatening crunch of leaves in the woods, what does it do? It freezes. For a moment it makes no movements, not even daring to breathe. It doesn't want any sensations to distract it from listening for that next crunch of leaves. If safety is perceived, the deer will move again, release its breath, and resume normal breathing as it returns to its browsing. Or, if danger is recognized, its body floods with responses, its breathing becomes rapid, and with a spring into action, it goes bounding away. Holding your breath at such moments is instinctive. I'm sure you gasp and hold your breath at the height of suspense when watching a horror movie, and you may also do it when caught up in any real-life emergency. Women frequently hold their breath in concentration when they put on their make-up. Men do it when shaving. When people think they're going to be told something unpleasant, they may instinctively try to stop their body's emotional reaction by stopping their breath.

However, a child can learn to make holding his breath a chronic condition, as if he is always in immediate danger, always in need of suppressing all emotions that might distract him from a state of prolonged concentration. A constant state of wariness is unhealthy and produces chronic muscular and emotional tension that powerfully inhibits the personal aliveness of your voice.

Try to recapture a sense of what your natural Body Breathing was like—and can be again. Imagine your breathing and the sound of a real belly laugh, like Santa on Christmas Eve, bursting out of you uncontrollably, tears streaming down your cheeks, "a laugh not of the face and diaphragm only, but of the whole man from head to heel."[1] A laugh like that takes up your entire body. In a quieter, even

---

[1] Thomas Caryle, *Sartor Resartus* (New York: The Odyssey Press, 1937), p. 33.

more complete way, your daily pattern of breathing should likewise engage your whole body.

You may have been exposed to other patterns of breathing recommended or touted in sports, dancing, jogging, or yoga, and wonder if they have anything to offer for managing tension or improving the expressiveness of your voice. For example, many cyclists are now experimenting with a reversed breathing rhythm in which instead of sucking air in and letting it go, you push the air out with a progressive flattening of your stomach and then let it back in. Yogis practice several types of deep breathing to loosen the diaphragm. Swimmers, who often develop harder muscles in the diaphragm area, keep their breathing high in the chest, using an efficient pattern of short, fast breaths. Weightlifters have their own ideas about how to integrate inhalations and exhalations with the demands on their muscles when they curl, cling, and press. Modern dancers often try for a spontaneity in which the dance movements take their impulse from the breath. Ballet dancers, on the other hand, frequently learn ways to close down the breath for greater muscle control in unnatural body alignments.

However, Body Breathing is the best way to breathe for your normal daily life and speaking voice. Unlike most types of breathing disciplines, Body Breathing is meant to be practiced every day, every hour, every minute, until it becomes a natural, unconscious part of your life, just as it was when you were an infant. You inhale and exhale a lot in the course of a day. If you breathe in and out about ten times a minute, that's six hundred times an hour, and close to fifteen thousand times a day. That's quite an opportunity to practice, and means if you're conscientious, you can learn to Body Breathe in a short time and regain its benefits for your health, aliveness, and voice.

Body Breathing can bring you the following benefits:

It releases the energy of your physical aliveness and fills your system with more oxygen.

It gives your voice the support of the biggest muscles in your body.

It gives you a strong sense of groundedness in moments of stress.

It will help bring emotion and expressiveness into your voice.

It may be hard for you to believe in or return to this natural way to breathe, especially if, like many people, you are somewhat overmentalized. The mind tends to resist the realization and experience that there is a wisdom in the body. It may take some reeducation and a change of heart to accept that change in your life and enhancement of your voice comes not so much by learning techniques or by some kind of intellectual knowledge, but by rediscovering your body's natural patterns. You will make progress as your breathing overcomes the resistance of your mind. Too much effort in learning new breathing patterns not only obstructs relaxation, but renders the breathing ineffective. It is a wonderful experience to finally let go of rigid, unemotional, thought-dominated patterns and to learn to trust your body and to enjoy the fullness of Body Breathing.

Breathing and De-Stressing

After our initial consultation, I began to see Julie and Frank separately. On the day of her first session with me, Julie came looking determined to change, but not sure of what direction to go in. She was wearing a severe dark suit and had her hair pulled back, as if this was her outfit for getting down to serious business. Her brown eyes darted about the room. I could tell she was all keyed up. It would turn out that this was her habitual style for dealing with change and growth—getting wound up like a tight spring in her own physical tension. This was her way of concentrating and focusing herself to meet demands and make superlative efforts. She was the type who pushed herself hard, rarely getting enough sleep, studying, preparing. She was aware of how much effort goes into achieving excellence, but not of how important a state of alert relaxation is to true efficiency and creativity. The result was that she looked fatigued almost all the time, and when she revved herself up for a big push, there was a feverish quality to her energy. She always completed her work on time, but every assignment and milestone tended to feel like a major panic, and the most frequent feedback she received was, "Hey, you look like you need a vacation!"

As with many people's habitual styles, Julie's had led her to some accomplishments, and, therefore, she tended to trust it. But since it was based on tension and, at times, hardly breathing, she was afraid to let go of it, afraid that relaxation would lead to inaction and failure. So she was locked into a limiting pattern that was of no help to her voice.

I asked her to lie down and make herself comfortable for the

De-Stresser Technique instruction. Her face expressed a slight sense of unsureness at having to approach her body in a more relaxed way. I could tell that she was trying hard to maintain her usual kind of rigid control. After we finished this first step, she was more calm and reassured. But then, as I showed her how to Body Breathe, another worry crossed her mind. She looked with misgivings at her loosened belt and laughed embarrassedly.

"Um, Body Breathing won't, uh, give me a big belly, will it?"

It was my turn to laugh. "No. You won't end up with a baby's paunch or Buddha belly. After all, it's not a big movement. It just feels big if you haven't been breathing this way."

Julie was used to a pattern of chronic muscular tension and shallow breathing that was a constant in every situation she experienced. I wanted to help her establish a new pattern in which Body Breathing was part of feeling more energized as well as more relaxed.

"You don't want to have a set rule in your mind, like, 'I should be breathing slowly' or 'I should be breathing deeply,'" I explained. "Find your natural rhythms. Let them be part of your entire body, and let them change and flow with you as you have your ups and downs during the day."

Over the next several weeks, Julie began to become aware of the ways in which she was tensed up. Parts of her body she had previously ignored she now realized were tight. She could feel how Body Breathing helped her gain sensation. And initially some of that sensation was tension. Eventually, Julie began to feel her resistance to releasing the tension, and with that, she had an experience that made her understand why deep breathing had caused her to feel nervous and sometimes tearful.

One day about a month into our work, as she was going through the De-Stresser Technique and Body Breathing in preparation for the Body Sounds, she began to tremble slightly.

"I'm just as tense as can be," she said.

"What would happen if you let that go?" I asked.

"Ha!" she added. "I'd make a fool of myself."

"Would you?" I prodded.

I could see her wince, as she struggled with herself. I could guess the nature of that struggle. She had reached her limit as far as trying to Body Breathe and improve her voice without letting herself relax. Now, I encouraged her to continue gently with deeper Body Breathing for a few moments and to add the sensory perception that she was melting into the floor more and more with each exhalation.

"Don't worry about getting it right," I said gently. "Don't worry about your voice right now. Just enjoy the melting."

Then, with her next exhalation, Julie began to softly cry. For a few moments the tears ran down her cheeks. Then, she took a big breath and I could see, for the first time, the tension really flow out of her body as she exhaled. Just as softly, she began to laugh.

"What a day," she said. "What a life."

"And what a voice," I added.

With the release of her tension through the Body Breathing, Julie's voice began to flow, without any of the hesitancy that had chopped her sentences. Even the small simple phrases with which she was now expressing her relief and sense of discovery had a sustained, expressive, alive quality.

"You released your tension from a much deeper level just then," I said. "You sound great."

"I finally let go," she said. "I really did it. I let go, and I began to have this good feeling of warmth and wholeness."

"Where?" I asked.

She looked at me with a deep, quiet joy shining in her eyes. "Here," she replied, generally motioning just below her navel and over her lower torso. "All my tightness seemed to flow out of me. I cried because it felt so good to experience myself so completely— with such a full, fresh newness."

"Well," I smiled back. "Body Breathing can seem to have a rejuvenating effect. When you speak in a more complete way with full breathing, your voice is constantly sending a healthy vibration throughout your body. This has a healing effect. Maybe this is one reason why voice teachers have greater longevity than people in other professions."

There was still more time left in our session, so I told Julie to continue by connecting this deeper relaxation to her work with the Body Sounds to see how much fuller and richer they would be now.

"And when you leave today," I said earnestly, "there's a lot I'd like you to think about. Today you really saw the connection between your Body Breathing, your chronic physical tension, and your voice. I know you feel good about it. There's a feeling of exhilaration that comes with this kind of breakthrough. But remember: you want to feel this relaxed and free every day. You want your voice to be expressive all the time, just as it is today. This means you still need to give conscious attention to encourage yourself to Body Breathe so you can make it a natural part of your life. It's great to breathe properly and release your voice when you're here with me, but the real effectiveness comes from using it day in and day out. You can have these benefits long beyond the defined period of time you work with me. It can serve you well the rest of your life."

Julie sat calmly, watching me with alert, smiling eyes. A smile tugged at her lips. She said in a relaxed, encouraging tone, "Definitely. Every day!"

Breathing and Emotion

Meanwhile I continued working with Frank. His voice lacked power. The way he spoke quickly, breathed shallowly, and became absorbed in self-reflections without a sense of communicating to the listener indicated to me some kind of long-standing block in his ability to use his voice as a means of expressing his feelings and personality. Something was making Frank hold back without his realizing it. Therefore, as I guided him through the De-Stresser Technique and Body Breathing, I encouraged Frank to explore his vocal history.

After several weeks, Frank began to have insight into the sources of his style of communication.

"I was thinking," he said, "about what caused my current problems. It was mostly influences when I was at school and with friends, and then even later on at work. I was put in school at an earlier age than most kids; so I was young for my class. I wasn't as tall or big as the other boys, and I was always trying to catch up physically with them. I remember sticking my chest out to look brave and strong. I guess some of that stayed with me as part of my idea of how a professional is to supposed to behave. There are times when I pretend a confidence I don't really feel."

"I understand you very well," I replied. "The way you hold your body so stiffly and the way you restrict your breathing are very much parts of your past history that have created ways for you to keep up your guard. In fact, your type of rigidity, posture, and shallow breathing is a common response many people have to cultural pressures."

As we talked, I asked Frank to stand in front of a mirror so he could look at the way he held his body. From one perspective, his posture was perfect. In our society, there is an idealized view of masculine strength—broad chest and shoulders and flat abdomen, chest out, belly in. This is true for both men and women. Men are praised for a rigid, military bearing ("Suck in that gut!") and women are expected to flatten their tummies with exercise or constrain themselves in control-top panty hose.

This posture, with its pulled in, hardened diaphragm, which forces you to breathe in your upper chest, is a cultural bias encouraged by magazines and TV images. The change from the natural Body Breathing of infants to the constrained breathing of adults is in line with our present emphasis on an image with an expected body type, at the expense of a certain breath and body energy flow.

"Even so," I said, "I think there's a part of your vocal problem that does come from your family."

"Well," Frank reconsidered, "I can remember having some impressions as a kid of my mother's and father's voices. My mother's voice is very musical—like a bird. My father's is gruff, but in a funny, kindly way."

"It's not just the sound of their voices you should consider," I said, "but the whole impact of their communication style. It's also essential to look at how your family expressed or dealt with emotions."

As Frank thought back more on his childhood, he remembered how his family had never been good at expressing anger.

"My mother never got angry," he said. "I mean, she never yelled and screamed or threw things. Instead, she would direct it into flurries of activity. I remember that once my father was late for dinner, and I had the feeling that there was something else going on. My mother didn't say an angry word or raise her voice. She just stayed in the kitchen, and cooked—and cooked. I have never seen anyone put so much energy into making a meal."

"And she probably held her breath," I commented.

"Probably. In fact, thinking back now, I remember the only sound she would make, besides the clanging of the pots and pans and doors, was a sharp, almost hissing intake of breath. Not a word, just that quick breath. Let me tell you, that was one angry sound. And she refused to ask for help. In fact, none of us kids would have dared said a word or entered the kitchen. By the time all the food was on the table, I just stared at every dish as if it were going to explode from all the energy she had put into it. My father didn't say a word.

We just started eating. I'll never forget when I first had to speak to ask someone to pass me something. My voice came out in a choked whisper like I had just swallowed my chewing gum."

"What about your father?" I asked.

Frank just shook his head. "My father wasn't much for raising his voice either. He was the kind who got quiet and stiff-lipped when he was angry, and only chuckled mildly when he was amused. He loved classical music and creating a peaceful atmosphere at home."

What Frank was describing was a certain kind of household where certain emotional expressions were frequently suppressed. The tone of Frank's voice had something of both his mother's musical voice and his father's gruff, humorous one. The expressiveness of Frank's voice was another matter. He had picked up a very tense, rigid way of holding himself and breathing, influenced by his parent's narrow range of emotional communication.

"Of course," said Frank, "I think I'm a lot more open and expressive than they were. I've worked hard to be successful, but I've enjoyed the stimulation and challenge, too. I like to laugh at jokes, stand up for my beliefs, and let people know how I feel. Until now, I hadn't really thought about my voice or communication style as inexpressive."

"Those early years exert a long-lasting, powerful influence on you," I told him. "Even though you're more willing and able to feel and express emotion, you and your voice need to be trained to reveal that emotion."

With his new insight into the influences of his past, Frank understood more deeply what he was trying to achieve by learning to Body Breathe. He was on the lookout now for the ways he held and controlled his body. In each subsequent session, he became better at allowing his throat to relax, his chest to release, and his lower body to move freely as he Body Breathed. Just as he had long ago found his own style of thinking, different from his father's, now he worked out a more natural way for his muscles to move as he began to learn Body Speaking. He was able to free his throat and chest muscles that were locked up rigidly like his father's. Gradually, the rhythms of his Body Breathing replaced the tight, fearful grip on his lower body that he had learned as a child in the presence of his mother's suppressed anger. Now, his own voice became more flexible. His breathing was no longer that of the boy who had to pretend he was brave. His voice was now appropriate for the secure adult he had become. Frank's rate of speaking slowed down as his breathing deepened and as the chest-out-belly-in rigidity of his body was replaced with a more natural, comfortable posture. With that handled, he had much better confidence, and his voice had greater power.

Frank discovered that he truly enjoyed this change. His voice was no longer something to be hidden. He now enjoyed communicating with other people, and as a result, his awareness and concern for his listeners increased dramatically. He became more sensitive to the reactions of the people he talked to.

"Everyone tells me I've become a much better conversationalist," he said.

"And how do you feel about it?" I asked.

"I feel like I've escaped from a trap," he said thoughtfully. "I think I had a fairly good sense of myself, but I was not aware how much more I could communicate that to other people. Now I can tell that I'm actively engaging my friends and associates when I talk to them. It makes me feel much more effective when I work, and much, much more alive."

"That sense of self will increase as you continue to master even more aspects of the BodyVoice concept," I assured him.

"That's great to look forward to," said Frank with a relaxed and expressive smile.

Feet on the Ground

As my work with Julie and Frank progressed, I began to see them together as a team to prepare them for their next training courses. At one point, Julie was scheduled to give a course in Dallas in two weeks, and the following week Frank was booked for Chicago. Naturally, they both had one question on their minds: Would the work they had done with me help them at their next public speaking engagements?

One thing was certain: Their voices and communication styles had improved dramatically, and so had their interaction as a team. Gone were Julie's distracting pauses and Frank's self-absorption. Both sounded and acted so much more self-assured and aware of their personal sources of power. I was sure that when they stood before their next training course audiences, they would discover that one of the greatest benefits of the techniques they were learning is how it settles and grounds you. Groundedness literally means having your legs firmly on the ground, supporting you. It's not just a mental state that tells you things are under control, or that you've got a clear sense of what you're doing, or that you're feeling confident. All these states of feeling securely at home with yourself are the benefits of having your body securely supported. And if your body is not, all that lovely mental stability and clarity is likely to disintegrate and fly to pieces with the first wave of fear or nervousness in a stressful situation. Julie, you will recall, had tried all sorts of mental preparations for her talks, but none of those techniques had helped her in the clinch. Body Breathing and using the support of your lower body, however, helps you gain strength from the strongest muscles of your body. When you're grounded, you're also a lot less likely to mentally space out, getting lost in abstraction. Paradoxically, when you most need to speak clearly, articulately, and persuasively, you do best not to think about your vocabulary and verbal abilities, but to relax and rely on your inner personal intention, which can best be supported by the natural, self-confident aliveness of your body. Then your words will flow.

"Well, I guess this is it," said Julie, a few days before she was scheduled to depart. "I feel relaxed now. Let's see what happens when I face the class."

Shortly after Julie returned from giving her course in Dallas, and Frank from Chicago, I met them to review their experiences. Julie was smiling as she entered the room and sat down, this time taking a seat in a straight-back chair, where she sat upright, looking relaxed, proud, and happy. Frank took the cozy armchair this time, sitting comfortably, breathing evenly and looking alert.

"Yes," Julie said to my unspoken question. "It went well. For both of us."

"It was a very rewarding experience," Frank agreed.

"Well, tell me," I urged them on.

Julie and Frank exchanged glances, then Julie began.

"I was nervous at first," she said. "The class was in a big open work area where all the word processing stations were set up. There was some mix-up in the schedule, and we had to combine two classes. Right away I saw I would be facing twice as many people as I had expected—just what I needed to hear! As soon as people took their seats, I began to feel the tension. It started right in my stomach. Someone asked me how long the course would take, and when I answered, I heard myself pause in midsentence.

"So, even as I handed out notebooks and 'courseware,' I began to use the De-Stresser Technique, just observing my arms and legs as I moved about, and making sure I was Body Breathing. It took about thirty seconds of concentration—and faith. But sure enough, I allowed myself to get underneath that fluttering in my stomach, and right down into my hips, I felt my knees relax, and I could sense my feet planted firmly on the floor. And, Joan, before I even realized what I was doing, I turned to the class, looked at them one by one, straight in the eye, and with a big smile, because I really felt confident, I said, 'So, are we ready to whip this system or what?' No hesitancy. No midsentence pause."

Julie reflected seriously. "The rest of the course was great. Usually, I'm so physically wound up, I come on like a freight train and collapse every night, and count each day I can keep up the pace as a miracle. But this time, I really felt energized. I was calm and alert, enjoying everyone's energy. I'd always heard of instructors talking about teaching as stimulating and getting as much back from the students as they put in. But this was the first time I experienced it."

"Well, it obviously won't be the last," I said. "How did it go for you, Frank?"

He smiled. "I got off to a scary start, too. Just as I was setting up, the company training manager told me that their vice president of marketing was going to sit in to observe the first session. They might as well have put a ten-thousand-watt spotlight on me and announced I was going to be on TV, live! My techniques really came to the rescue. As I did the course setup work, I was able to keep my sense of feeling grounded, like feeling very connected with the earth, right through the carpet and floor. But you should see the floor in that kind of high-tech work area—electric outlets, thick transmission cables, power distribution boxes, power stabilizers, *power* everywhere. I kept thinking, 'Just relax and keep Body Breathing, and you'll have your own power. And people will hear it.'"

Frank went on, "I could tell I was connecting well with the group. The days when I got lost in my own thinking without regarding my audience are long gone. Eyes were on me, faces smiled. And it was such a satisfaction to know I was expressing what I really felt inside. I knew the problems and pressures these people faced. I knew what my system could do and couldn't do. I sympathized and I wanted to help. And that's what I communicated.

"And my voice! One of the women tape recorded me. Boy, was I surprised. I sounded great."

"You both sound great," I said. "And you look great, too. You've both learned about the emotional, physical, and energetic benefits of Body Breathing, and how it becomes the foundation for Body Speaking. You've discovered on many levels how mastering *body* awareness and understanding *breathing* sheds a new light on *speaking*."

six
The Sexual Connection

She passed the phone booth, then circled back to it. Then she passed it again. Mr. Henderson had asked her to call back that afternoon for the final Yes or No. It's got to be Yes, she thought. A Yes would mean that she had been accepted as a junior partner in one of the city's most prestigious, respected law firms. She'd taken a late lunch so she'd be out of the City Hall office to make her call, but now she was scared.

As she walked, she caught her reflection in a store window—dark blond hair, blue business suit, serious face. She thought she looked professional and hoped she had come across that way at last week's meeting. She felt nervous and went into a card shop. There were many cards that caught her fancy, and she bought some for her folks, her best friend, and her husband Neil, a successful musical composer for recordings and films. She thought of him for a moment, his encouraging voice in her mind, "Hey, they're going to love you." Then she walked back to the phone booth—and continued on. An ice cream parlor tempted her. No, let's keep that weight off. She went back to the phone booth and started going through her purse for change.

She was afraid to call. What if she didn't get the nod? Her knees were trembling. This was such a good opportunity. It would mean a major career move as an attorney, doing work she respected and making the money she deserved, her big step out of the government and into the private sector. But if she didn't get it . . . Her eyes wandered across the street to a charming dress boutique. What a gorgeous suit!

104

A voice inside her began a familiar litany: "Good, Sandra. You don't know whether you're going to get this job yet, and you're ready to go on a shopping spree. You should have more self-control. You ought to be more together. You should—"

Stop right there! She recognized those Should's and Ought To's. It was her Attacking Voice. And as quickly as she could, she used the Process of Disengaging. She used the method of Exaggeration. "Sure," she retorted to herself, "I'm the only one in the world who gets jazzed up about buying something I can't afford."

She punctuated the good feeling of disengaging from her Attacking voice by putting coins in the slot and dialing the number. As she dialed, she realized she was unconsciously holding her breath.

No! I can keep Body Breathing—gently, naturally. I can use the De-Stresser Technique. I can manage my breath to manage this tension. Oh, yes. What's going on in my arms and legs? To her surprise, they were not turning into jelly like they used to in tense situations. She felt a sense of weight and solidity, and then slowly, surely, energy and confidence. She felt herself inhale deeply into her lower body, and a warm, secure feeling stirred. She let her aware-ness rest for a moment on the sensation in her genitals, and self-assurance began to flow through her body.

The phone line was ringing, and then a voice answered.

"Hello," she said. She was smiling now, and feeling earnest and clear. "Rachel? This is Sandra Brady, calling back for Mr. Henderson."

Her voice sounded purposeful and confident.

"Oh, Sandra," came the eager reply, "I'm so glad you called."

A moment later Mr. Henderson was on the line. His first words to her were, "How does coming on board with us on Monday sound?"

Sandra felt waves of relief and excitement flowing through her body. As soon as she had accepted the position, she quickly made a second phone call to her husband.

"Neil? Guess what?"

There wasn't a moment's hesitation in his voice.

"You got the junior partnership." He chuckled in his special way that she always recognized as his happiness for her.

"How did you know?"

"It's the *way* you said it," he laughed. "The sound of your voice. That was the most triumphant 'Guess what?' I've ever heard from you."

Everything You Always Wanted To Know

Sandra had worked with me about three months, steadily bringing out greater confidence and aliveness in her voice, when her career began to open up for her. Did it surprise you that as part of sensing her body to relax and get focused, she paid attention to the sensations in her genitals? It's important for you now to take a moment and explore your reactions to this part of Sandra's story. Did you find it refreshing? Embarrassing? Disturbing? Intriguing? Did you think, "Yes, stay in touch with your body's sexual aliveness. That will help you feel more grounded and secure. That will help you feel your own personal power." Or did you find it strange that someone about to make an important business call should consciously direct attention to this area of the body?

The aliveness of your voice and the overall vitality of your body draw on many internal pools of energy—for instance, your muscular energy, your emotional energy, and, often overlooked, your sexual energy. Many people think about sexuality in a very limiting way, as if sexual aliveness were only a matter of responding to sexual attraction or engaging in sexual activity. But when I talk about sexual energy in the context of the BodyVoice concept, I am not referring to sexual interest or arousal, but to a crucially important component of your overall body energy:

> Sexual or energetic aliveness is one of the energies of the lower body that is an important source of your natural vitality, creativity, and power. It can be experienced as a sense of health, well-being, and aliveness throughout your entire body and in the sound of your voice.

An understanding of these broader, full-body aspects of sexual-energetic aliveness will give you insight into some of the ways this energy can help you in the following important aspects of your professional and personal life:

> Developing the qualities in your vocal sound that express your most personal, attractive dimensions.

> Achieving and expressing emotional and personal maturity, beginning with communication habits and vocal changes at puberty.

> Exploring issues in marriages and serious relationships that are affected by men's and women's perceptions of their partners' voices.

Growing through fears of vulnerability and self-sufficiency that can inhibit the aliveness of your voice.

Attractive People, Attractive Voices

Men and women spend an astounding amount of energy, money, and intelligence on clothes, jewelry, makeup, and hairstyles, and put great store on the attitudes and behaviors considered sexually sophisticated. But a person's beautiful, charming, or virile appearance may only achieve an initial kind of attractiveness unless he or she can experience, enjoy, and communicate an inner, healthy, sensuously alive quality. You can hear it in Debra Winger's expressively husky voice, in Marilyn Monroe's lush breathiness, and in Jaclyn Smith's silky purr. You can feel it in the powerful personal magnetism of Paul Newman, the smooth fullness of Harry Hamlin, and the rich, seductive resonance of James Earl Jones. Having voices that combine all these attractive qualities is part of the lasting appeal of Yves Montand and Simone Signoret.

A person's voice can be a tip-off to the broader, more meaningful parts of a person's sexual-energetic aliveness. A man might respond to a woman across the room, but when she comes over to speak to him, his heart may sink because of some dull, harsh, or insincere quality in her voice. Or a woman might go weak in the knees over a great-looking man only to wince at the choked, self-centered way that he talks. A voice that stays close to a monotone, that makes you come across as too smooth an operator, or that in any way sounds dull, clumsy, or false can sabotage the most stunning wardrobe or alluring cologne. If your best "So how about dinner tonight?" sounds lifeless or contrived, you may not come across as appealing or desirable.

Let me give you an example of what a voice can sound like when it communicates a vital, thrilling sexual aliveness. There's a well-known broadcaster in San Francisco with a natural BodyVoice, and people just melt over the way he sounds. One day I was about to do a commercial with him, and he was in the sound booth. I said to the engineers and clients in the control room, "Where do you feel his voice in your body?"

They looked at me curiously at first, but I encouraged them to let themselves concentrate on the actual physical experience of listening to his voice. Some of them closed their eyes for a moment. Then they looked at me in some surprise.

Everyone agreed they felt his voice resonating mostly in their lower bodies in a sensuous way. It was low, rich, and sexually alive, with a powerful personal quality.

One of the clients shook her head. "You could go diving for pearls in a voice like that."

Conversely, I once worked with a famous actress whose body was extremely physically contracted with deep-rooted tension. She was the epitome of physical beauty, a photographer's dream come true. But her voice lacked the warm, deeply personal aliveness that really makes an audience respond fully to a performance. Despite her beauty, her tension-bound body was unable to convey the multi-faceted human qualities she should have been able to communicate.

What makes a voice have an enjoyable, appealing, sensuous quality? The key is the kind of relaxation and full Body Breathing that allows your complete physical aliveness to flow through your body from head to toe, unobstructed by muscular or emotional tension or rigidity. The healthy circulation of this energy should be experienced as an enjoyment of your entire body, and as a quality in your voice, but I've found that an effective way to keep in contact with this energy is to focus on a gentle awareness of your genitals as you go through your day.

Mistakenly, many people think it's natural and normal to have no sensation in the pelvis except during sexual activity. But the entire lower body should be alive and warm as part of your sexual-energetic awareness all the time. Children are often told not to look "down there," not to touch "there," not to feel "there," it's not appropriate to talk about "there." By the time they've grown up, they've learned not to feel any sensation "there." Certainly, many people are surprised at the idea of any kind of genital awareness in connection with carrying on an ordinary personal or business conversation.

Just do a simple check on yourself right now. Ask yourself if you are aware of any kind of feeling in your genitals, any sense of their presence at all. If you are not aware of any sensation, it's unlikely that you're sufficiently relaxed, that you're Body Breathing fully, or that your body energies are circulating as freely and fully as they could be. This could mean that you are not in touch with yourself as deeply and responsively as you might be, and that your voice is probably not at its best.

Carl was a literary agent who found out during a session with me just how effective it was to monitor his genitals as a cue to whether he was speaking with his BodyVoice or letting his vocal sound fall off. He was telling me how confident he felt this particular morning about speaking at an upcoming writer's workshop and about videotaping it for me. As a beginning student with me, he was still learning to educate himself about the accuracy of his perceptions of his performance and his perceptions regarding the sound of his voice. When we played back the video, he was stunned at the lack of body presence, eye contact, and spontaneous energy.

Carl took a moment to focus on his body, after watching the playback, and he realized that he had no awareness of any sensation below his midsection. When I asked him where his genitals were during the taping, he smiled sheepishly and said "I think Topeka, Kansas."

"Well," I laughed, "It might be a good idea to invite them back."

This check on genital awareness is an effective way to keep in touch with your energetic presence and aliveness, especially important when you're at work. Many corporations invest substantial time and money in management and organization development seminars to increase staff flexibility and productivity, and to help managers and employees at every level find greater efficiency and satisfaction in their working experiences. But talking about flexibility, creativity, openness, and interpersonal sensitivity can be just talk, unless you have a way of experiencing the underlying body awareness that makes these goals realizable. For example, managers are often advised to personalize their dealings with their boss and associates. But how can you do this in a way that is not contrived or counterproductive? You can share your personal energy, your aliveness, which can be communicated powerfully by the sound of your BodyVoice. Keeping in contact with your body's sexual component of aliveness—and checking on the level of your genital awareness—can help you transform and personalize your work experience in an appropriate way.

Developing your BodyVoice can help you release the natural flow of healthy sexual energies throughout your entire body. You've probably had experiences of this body flow during times you've fallen in love. Allowing these energies to flow on a daily basis is like signalling your body that it's okay to fall in love with itself. It's not unusual, then, for your enjoyment of sexuality to improve. I've seen this happen enough times that I'm not surprised when someone who's worked with me for a while comes in with a smile and says, "Well, I don't know why, but my sex life is sure getting better." But it's also common for someone to realize that a relaxed awareness of sexual aliveness can improve all aspects of life.

Allen, who thought he would always be the one to put his foot in his mouth, whether trying to make polite small talk with a client or approaching someone on the dance floor, realized that it was when he was living in his head, cut off from his body energy, that he made his worst bloopers. On the contrary, when he let go and was comfortable with his body and the energy of his sexuality, he found that he had a much greater sense of appropriateness, sensitivity to social nuance, and spontaneously apt expression.

So much of living could be more meaningful, stimulating, and fulfilling if you don't overmentalize yourself. You'll be more creative and outgoing if you are more in contact with your sexual energies as part of your overall physical aliveness.

From the Female Perspective

The process of releasing the aliveness of your sexual energy into your voice is basically the same for men and for women. But there are some issues that are special for women, starting at puberty.

Like many rites of passage in our culture, there is no ritual to mark the growing maturity of a woman's voice. For the most part, it is assumed that once a woman's body has matured, so has her voice. But this is not always the case. Women don't experience the dynamic changes in their vocal cords during puberty that men do. They don't develop an Adam's apple and their vocal cords don't physiologically change in such a dramatic way. The adult woman's voice develops gradually, less noticeably. Sometimes the vocal change doesn't happen at all. Unresolved sexual and identity issues that arise during childhood and adolescence can possibly be the causes for a woman to have a high, little-girl voice, even once her body has fully matured.

Frequently, a woman's girlishness, her air of virginity or innocence, relates back to the family influences that can shape many aspects of her voice—her vocal history. Usually, women with this problem had their girlishness overly admired, or they were afraid to move on to more adult femaleness. It's normal to enjoy having feelings of being Daddy's little girl or to have some fear of competing with your mother. But these should be passing phases. If not, a woman may try to stay young and sexless in her appearance, her mannerisms, and her voice.

There are enough variations of this common problem that you may be facing some aspect of it in your life. Even if your voice is not noticeably high-pitched, breathy, or cute, you may still feel shy or uncomfortable about letting your voice fully express the power and sexual aliveness of your adult body. One woman I know experienced a great deal of resistance in learning to Body Breathe and develop her Body Voice. Finally, with much agitation, she came right out and told me, "I don't want my voice to sound sexy." A vibrant alive sound that reflected her full adult womanliness frightened her. This was partly because she needed to learn how to feel more grounded. In *The Body Reveals*, Kurtz and Prestera point out:

> To mobilize and move with flow would mean allowing free energy through the body, and this is more energy that can structurally or emotionally be handled. To avoid falling apart, he or she blocks [the] flow.[1]

Her fear also owed much of its hold on her to our cultural expectations around male and female roles.

In our culture, there are certain men who fall in love with little-girl types who have little-girl voices. Corrine was an attractive, sylphlike diet clinician who ran afoul of one such male. Scott was a wealthy hospital administrator who treated beautiful young women like ornaments. After every ten or so years of marriage, he was ready to replace his wife with a newer model, because his spouse with the young voice no longer had a young body. He was passionate and generous when he was trying to win Corrine, but eight years later, he moved on to someone younger, just as he had twice before.

I've seen men's reactions to a woman's little-girl voice work the other way, too. Howard and Michelle were high school sweethearts who ran into marriage problems in their late twenties because of Michelle's Shirley Temple voice. As Howard's career advanced, he began to feel a growing sense of disenchantment with what he thought was Michelle's lack of maturity. In his mind, she was still

---

[1]Ron Kurtz and Hector Prestera, M.D., *The Body Reveals* (New York: Harper and Row, 1976), p. 40.

acting or sounding like a little girl instead of a full-fledged woman. Ironically, Michelle had matured emotionally along with Howard, but her voice had remained the same. This relationship came perilously close to divorce when Howard became infatuated with a woman at work who seemed more on his level of accomplishment. Fortunately, Michelle finally thought to work on her voice. As she began to sound more mature, Howard was able to cast off the erroneous impression of her character he had formed based on her little-girl voice and see that in fact they were growing in complementary ways.

For another type of woman, the little-girl voice represents a fear of displeasing or angering the important people in her life. Lacking in the self-confidence that comes from healthy sexual aliveness, she is often submissive to men who admire her air of cuteness and take advantage of the timid, placating behaviors that go with it. A woman caught in this pattern may have learned both her way of handling relationships and her vocal characteristics from unconsciously holding onto her childhood imitation of her mother's voice and mannerisms, inhibiting her from discovering her own budding vocal identity. Frequently, the release of her Body-Voice brings with it a big step forward in emotional maturity and confidence in her adult individuality.

Millie was a pretty, petite woman whose life for many years was shaped around her husband's needs and expectations. She had jet black hair and dark eyes, and her lips always seemed to hold a smile. Her voice had the cheerful, piping quality of a good-natured child only too happy to accommodate anyone for attention and affection in return. But inside, she was feeling trapped and resentful.

"I don't say anything to him about my feelings," she told me, "because it would sound ridiculous. Everything I say comes out sounding adorable—even if I'm livid with rage or sad enough to cry. He'll never think I need anything more than a pat on the head."

As Millie developed a deeper, beautiful voice, she began to feel a strength and self-confidence appropriate to an intelligent, refined woman. One day she stood up to her husband, and for the first time her anger did not sound cute and dismissable. He was suddenly forced to recognize her true needs as a serious challenge to his domineering role in their relationship. I hadn't suggested to Millie that this might happen, because I don't like to program anyone's expectations. I wanted Millie to have the freedom to evolve, and I was delighted that she was doing so well. In the following months Millie found that not only her husband, but many of the special people in her life, who were used to her as a meek, fluffy, sweet person, were disconcerted to find that there was an assertive side to her.

Another communication issue that can come up in a marriage or serious relationship is when a woman finds herself up against a man who refuses to talk enough on an emotional level. Laurie was a young saleswoman whose marriage began to founder in her husband Doug's macho silence. It was a common thing for them, she told me, to have a terrible fight in which Doug yelled at her to leave him alone, but never explained what he was feeling or what he thought about the interpersonal issues she had raised.

"'Speak to me!' I would scream. And he would just walk away," she told me. "I'd give up on the marriage, convinced he was going to leave me. Then, the next day, he'd call from work, sounding friendly and cheerful, and say, 'So, how's Chinese food sound tonight?'—as if nothing had happened."

Women frequently have a wider, more comfortable emotional vocabulary than men do. Men are often encouraged during childhood to hold back their emotions and to keep their tears and emotional words to themselves. They learn to equate manliness with strong but silent responses and with refusing to discuss issues charged with feeling. Some men think it's more mature to remain silent during an argument, not giving in to emotional exploration. It takes courage and understanding on the part of many men to open up their feelings, and women who suffer from having a silent partner should note that the man rarely holds back just to be difficult or mean; he is more likely a prisoner of his own family and cultural vocal history. If a man comes to me to work on his voice, he may discover that Body Breathing and the relaxation of his contracted muscles frees his emotional energy. With an enhanced sense of sexual aliveness and a more expressive vocal quality, he may discover the satisfaction of communicating openly about his feelings.

There are many patterns both men and women can fall into when they don't have a sense that they can communicate fully. Rosalind, a tough country woman from Kentucky, came to see me for some help with her voice. She was part-owner of a neighborhood fruits and vegetables store with a reputation for having some of the finest produce in the city. Now married to her third husband, she told me she wouldn't put up with any nonsense from a man. Referring to the fallout of one especially heated argument with her husband, she said, "I didn't talk to him for three days."

I asked her why she considered this strategy effective, and the answer was, "I was mad. That'll show him."

You may know someone like Rosalind who has perfected the silent treatment and cold shoulder, or who does the opposite: expresses anger and frustration with a spate of rapid-fire words, aiming their verbal machine gun at their victim's psyche. Both patterns—talking too little and too much—are poor substitutes for truly personal, meaningful communication with an expressive BodyVoice. From my work with her, I knew that Rosalind had great difficulty expressing her emotions. Her models of relationships were ones filled with frustration, and it was hard for her to experience the gentle flow of her sexual-energetic aliveness. The muscular and emotional tensions in her body were like logs and rocks damming a river that should have been flowing smoothly. When she learned to release some of her emotional obstructions, she was able to let more of the warm, sensitive quality of her sexual aliveness into her voice. She also found it was a lot better to express her anger strongly, clearly, and honestly, rather than storming off as a way of punishing her husband.

The state of your sexual-energetic aliveness depends a lot on how free or inhibited your Body Breathing movement is, and on how various emotional and physical energy blocks have arranged themselves in your upper and lower body. Like a magician doing the trick of sawing the woman in half, you may be using midbody tension to cut the flow of your mind-body communication. Releasing that tension, and Body Breathing, can restore a sense of aliveness both to your lower body and to your chest, throat, voice, and mind.

It may not have occurred to you that this unobstructed flow of full-body energetic aliveness is important for you at work. But if you allow the silent magician inside you to saw you in half, your powers of mental clarity and creativity can become cut off from their sources of energy and support in your lower body. This is not a healthy or productive state for women or men. And how can you tell if your sexual aliveness is blocked? Focus on your thighs, lower spine, buttocks, genitals, and lower abdomen, and then you'll begin to discover whether you're in touch with the most powerful sources of your personal energy, or whether you need to make that inner magician of your new awareness put your two halves back together.

From the Male Perspective

I generally have at any particular time as many men working with me on their voices as I do women, and I appreciate some of the special concerns and discoveries men have with their voices and their bodies.

Men go through major physiological vocal changes at puberty. The cracking of a young boy's voice when the changes begin is a cute phase, but once the deeper voice is there, some boys go through another phase in which they are embarrassed by the way they sound. Brian, who is now a local newscaster on radio, told me that when his voice changed at puberty, it seemed to become so big and rich that everything he said sounded like the thunder of a holy pronouncement or the introduction to a death-defying circus act.

"I was just a kid sitting at the dinner table. But when I'd say, 'Please pass the potatoes,' the words came out like cannon fire."

For months, Brian was afraid to say anything for fear it would seem ridiculous.

"I thought that everything I said had better be intelligent or earth-shaking in significance. My voice certainly made it sound that way."

Brian's family reacted positively to his mature voice, and he slowly gained confidence in his adult sound. However, many boys whose voices become dramatically deeper at puberty become abashed and develop an overly quiet, suppressed vocal style. A boy at this stage needs the support and understanding of his family. It helps to have parents who can recognize his vocal changes at puberty and nurture his new voice. Brian certainly owed some of his later vocal confidence to the way his parents told him he was bright and that his big voice was wonderful.

Most men with good voices are as proud of them as a peacock of its feathers. Men whose voices are not naturally deep and powerful may try overly hard to achieve what they consider a vocal sound worthy of their manhood. Ian was the physical epitome of the ideal masculine build. Corporate tax consultant by day, amateur body-builder by night, Ian went at his voice the same way he took on an audit or pumped iron. When he came to me, he had an impressive voice—loud, growling, but not full and resonant, and frequently hoarse. Physically, he kept the muscles of his throat tensed, as though he were trying to make his voice bulge like his biceps. His jaw was tight and hard as a linebacker's face mask, and his chin thrust forward. My work with Ian led him to see how he was trying to speak in a way that actually imprisoned this voice, mistaking muscular holding in his neck and midsection as the source of his vocal power.

Ian learned how to let more flowing energy through his hard muscles and into his inner energetic places as he began to breathe more fully. He became more aware of how the vise of tension around his midsection restricted his breathing, cutting his body in half and obstructing the full circulation of his sexual-energetic aliveness. In fact, he was amazed at just how specific and deep the relaxation could go. One day, he started a session with me by announcing that he had been swimming and was feeling quite free and loose. But as he was doing the De-Stresser Technique, he suddenly laughed.

"Wow—guess what just happened? And I thought I was relaxed! I just felt my testicles slide down. I didn't even realize they were contracted."

As the weeks passed, his throat, jaw, and lower body began to release more and more and gain greater mobility. Ian learned to enjoy the flow of this healthy energy throughout his body, and his voice gradually developed more of the real power he wanted without his having to force it.

Some men, on the other hand, perhaps overly conscious that they aren't going to reach a certain muscular, physical image, also abandon their voices as an expression of male pride and power. Phillip was a young, slight-bodied mathematician and science-fiction afficionado who placed his pride in his mental talents and vicariously enjoyed physical male prowess only in literary fantasies of heroes conquering empires on alien worlds. His girlfriend urged him to see someone about his voice because of an annoying speaking habit he had developed. Conversation with Phillip was a trial, because he let his sentences dribble off into inaudibility. Phillip talked as though his thoughts were mathematical calculations that he could truncate before he reached the final decimal place.

When as part of our initial interview I asked him what he felt about his voice, the answer I received was, "I'm here as part of a general self-improvement thing that could, um, . . ."—and all the projection went out of his voice so that I could barely hear the last words of what he was saying.

When I pointed out to him how this habit severely limited the effectiveness of his communication, he said, "I know my voice isn't powerful, but I'm not going to bray so that people think I'm the Warlord of Zar."

I laughed with him. "No, forcing your throat isn't what I had in mind. You need to Body Breathe to charge up your emotional vitality and energetic aliveness."

Phillip zealously worked with me on the physical and emotional blocks that caused his vocal withdrawal. He began to find more power in his voice and a greater feeling of vitality. As a result, he began to enjoy communicating a personal sense of his own special masculinity. The following year, he found that there was an outlet for the expression of his more powerful personal presence: He was in great demand as a panelist at science-fiction conventions, and audiences enjoyed hearing his speculations—and his delivery. After one convention Phillip called to tell me how exciting the change in his voice and body aliveness was for him.

"My throat didn't get hoarse, and my voice had more full projection than ever," he said. "And for the first time, I felt my entire body was energized."

"Where did that power in your voice come from?" I asked.

Phillip replied in a deep, rich voice, "It came right from my gonads."

Obviously, I was very pleased for him.

Men also sometimes fear that the muscular relaxation necessary to develop a BodyVoice might undermine their inner emotional toughness and strength. Martin was a young assistant district attorney who scoffed at the television archetype of the hard-boiled Tough Guy until he saw his own personal reactions to some harsh realities.

"Frankly, Joan," he told me, "When you've dealt with enough power politics, scams, and threats of violence, and have been in and out of enough courtrooms and jails, you want to be hard and tough inside—and you want to sound tough."

But Martin didn't feel tough inside, just numb and shut down, and he didn't sound tough, just harsh. Martin's work with me turned out to be a major growth experience for him. At first, he resisted relaxing and exploring his body sensations. The first few times he produced Body Sounds and realized that his voice could become softer, richer, and fuller, he felt threatened. The discovery of his more energetic aliveness was a sign he was moving beyond the uncomfortable but safe places he'd been operating from, and it scared him. He went through a phase in which he made excuses for cancelling sessions—"I've gotta travel more for my job" and "They're putting much more on my caseload. I'll have to stop for a while."

But as Martin became more practiced at all the aspects of the Kenley Method, his attitude began to change. He began to see strength, not in terms of petrified hardness, but in terms of mental and emotional agility, groundedness, and awareness. The richer, more vibrant, resonating sound of his voice began to feel more appropriate to him.

"I was in court yesterday," he said during one session with me, "on a kind of despicable case with a lot of shady characters and heavy legal challenges. I was able to stand up to the pressure and fight back. I didn't have to be an insensitive rock. I realized that there's more strength in accepting you have a sensitive, vulnerable core."

The acceptance of feelings of vulnerability and pleasure in the body is a stumbling block for some men. I worked a long time with Richard, a computer salesman who had earned a black belt in karate. The discipline and endurance required by this martial art appealed to him immensely. He told me of some of the tests he had taken, of doing three-hundred sit-ups, of demonstrating stances, kicks, and attacks, and taking on one opponent after another. When it came to doing my exercises, he found himself faced with an entirely different kind of struggle. It was usually only toward the end of our sessions that he managed to achieve any kind of relaxation and feeling of energy flow. When he went home, he returned to his karate and turned away from feelings of warmth, vulnerability, and pleasure. Richard stopped his sessions after a couple months and was one of the few people I simply could not get through to. His defenses were too strong and his fear too great.

Hardness, toughness, rigidity, invulnerability—these are some of the qualities that men frequently think are desirable facets of their masculinity, and so these things come through in their personalities, their bodies, and the sound of their voices. But allowing sexual-energetic aliveness can make a man's body and voice communicate a truly powerful, masculine identity.

For both men and women, the fragmenting of the body's natural harmony of energies causes many physical, emotional, and vocal problems. Your mind and body, your emotions, your breathing, your sexual-energetic aliveness, and your voice should work together, integrating all these aspects into a BodyVoice unity.

seven

The Finer Things

A beach at sunset: waves and sand and the colors of fire in the sky. As I drove past on my way home, I said to myself, "How magnificent, just like a postcard," and nearly continued on. But then I felt a pang of regret at the thought of letting it all go by so quickly. I parked, and took a short stroll, just as the sun sank behind the hills. Soon I was noticing a world of subtle beauties I would have missed if I had gone on my way: the rainbow hues in the frothy bubbles where the undertow pulls the waves back, the scurrying of the sandpipers, the scent of the air and the feel of the breeze, the infinite variety of the light caught up in the curling waves, now like glass, now like a serpent's glistening scales.

Later, I was dining out with two friends, one an artist, one a lawyer. Amidst the conversation about films and legal technicalities, my artist friend explained his ideas of how a writer or director creates the kind of character that seems to have a life of its own.

"You start with a basic direction," he said, "whether it calls for a man of action, a bad girl with a heart of gold, a greedy bad guy, a tragic hero, or an extraterrestrial that wants to phone home. Then you can focus all your talent and creativity on the intimate character details. You want to know his first woolly thoughts when he wakes up in the morning, and where he cuts himself when he's shaving, exactly how her face creases when she hears a smooth line, and which toes hurt when she takes her shoes off. Rich detail, physical and/or psychological. It fills things out, brings the character to life."

The lawyer, meanwhile, likened this perspective to his own interest in another kind of detail: going through every word of every clause in contracts he negotiated.

"Fine print," the artist kidded him.

"Believe me," said the lawyer, "knowing all the ins and outs and spotting any loopholes is what makes a carefully crafted contract as solid as a great character."

I listened, and I was thinking that all this was true about what it means to have a BodyVoice that reflects your personal identity, your charisma, your personal power. First, you develop your awareness and skills with the major components of your vocal sound—release from physical and emotional tension, Body Breathing, awareness of mind-body responses, and the flow of that healthy vitality I referred to as your sexual-energetic aliveness. But then, once you have a good grasp of the basics, it's important to go further and consider even more intimately the qualities that are part of being fully human, fully alive and dynamic—the finer things in your human experience that support and nourish your personal growth and success. I mean such things as that treasured sense of your own uniqueness, your creativity, your spiritedness that won't let adversity keep you down, your humor, anger, and loving contact with the world.

Tapping these energies, and understanding how they can enhance your life, is central to the teachings of some schools of self-development work. They can be referred to as *subtle energies*. Learning to experience them is a personal process of discovery which can be facilitated by the sensitive instruction and guidance of a private teacher, as well as through the supportive structure of workshops and seminars. I personally learned about this rewarding aspect of self-discovery from my own teacher, Dr. A. H. Almaas. These finer energies are an integral part of the BodyVoice concept. They are the qualities that you can get in touch with as you contact the more inner sensations of your body that give life and color to your voice.

The Energies of Aliveness

Becoming more finely in tune with your body awareness can lead to quite an adventure. In the same way that you can educate your ear to be more sensitive to the emotional qualities in your voice and in other people's voices, so you can also develop your sensory experience of your body to deepen and broaden your human capacity to participate wholly and consciously in life's amazing variety of struggles and pleasures.

What then are some of these finer body experiences that enliven and empower your voice? And where in your body can you make contact with them? The major ones I want to share with you here are:

Support—legs
Self-sufficiency—lower abdomen
Will power—solar plexus
Love and compassion—heart (chest)
Self-expression and creativity—throat
Mental clarity—mind (head)

These are felt mind-body-emotion experiences. When these finer energies are tapped, you can feel them operating throughout your entire body, you can hear them in the enriched qualities of your voice, and you can see the expanded perspective and power they bring to your life. When these energies are *not* accessed, you will feel quite differently—deficient, lacking for some reason that probably you wish you could put your finger on and start to change.

As a guide to some of the emotional-energetic body responses you may have as you develop your BodyVoice, look at the following chart. It will give you an overview of some of the experiences associated with the basic types of body energies when the essential energy of each body area is flowing, and when it is not.

Finer Energies and Qualities of Body Experiences

Center	Positive Experience	Negative Experience
Mind (Mental Clarity)	I feel clear	I am confused
Throat (Self-expression, creativity)	I can express myself	I can't express myself
Heart (Love, compassion)	I feel loving and open	I feel shielded and closed

Solar Plexus (Will power, determination)	I can do it	I can't do it
Lower Abdomen (Self-sufficiency, personal presence)	I am enough	I'm not enough
Lower Spine and Legs (Support)	I feel strong and supported	I feel weak and ungrounded

You will find, as we are about to discuss, that you can learn to open up yourself to these positive experiences. When you do release what was blocked or closed, you will have an experience of *joy* at the realization of each new capacity. Joy is an important ingredient by itself as well as an accompanying quality that comes with the actualization of support, self-sufficiency, compassion, creativity and clarity. It's a light, bubbling, sparkling sensation. Your life is dimmer when this quality is repressed. And it's an important part of yourself to contact for the aliveness of your vocal quality.

Let's run through the chart from bottom to top, seeing how it feels to be in contact with each of these energies—and how it feels to be out of contact with them. And let's see how it affects your voice, your communication, and your life.

Support—Legs

The muscular strength of your legs can give support to your voice, allowing you to relax your lower torso, chest and throat, which in turn helps you to release a more free, full-bodied vocal sound. But your legs also have a finer energy that can bring an experience of having all the support you need to go forward, to take purposeful steps in your life. When you experience this energy, you feel you could open any door, walk right in. You feel that you have the power to take action. You probably have a sense of this energy when you're striding confidently along, like John Travolta's character was filmed in *Saturday Night Fever*, strutting down the street, letting his legs take him where they would, communicating a feeling of active strength with every step. This experience can color all your actions. You can feel like the indefatigable investigative reporters on TV's "60 Minutes" who can find their way through any barrier to get their story and confront whatever truth awaits.

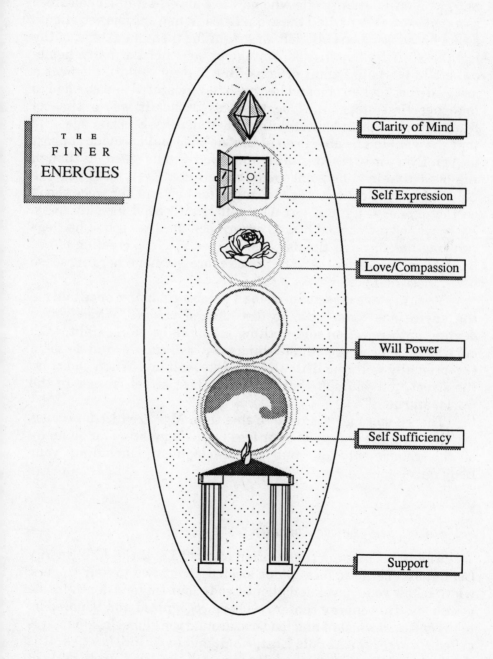

THE
FINER
ENERGIES

Clarity of Mind

Self Expression

Love/Compassion

Will Power

Self Sufficiency

Support

The qualities this gives your voice are sureness and strength. Margie, a former housewife who now has a well-established career as a real estate agent, had these qualities. When she showed clients around a house she really felt was right for them, her sense of the rightness of the match was contagious and helped many home-owners-to-be realize their dreams. But Margie could remember a few years back when she and her husband separated and she had to take her first steps into the business world. It was a time of traumatic change and questioning of her identity. She had a feeling that she wouldn't be able to do it, that no one would provide support for her. Every new responsibility made her feel fatigued, as though she needed to lean on someone or something. Even making some inquiring phone calls seemed too much for her, and her voice shook on the phone, weak and lost as a tuft of milkweed blowing away. Later, when she learned how to experience the strength of her legs carrying her through the day, she jumped into the creation of her business with both feet. And her voice expressed her emerging sense of firmness and power.

Myra, a stage director of a small theater company, once told me the advice she often gave to discouraged actors. "When you're dealing with rejection and nothing seems to be going right, take enjoyment in even the simple things you still can do, and do them exceptionally well, the little things—like walking. When you cross the street, tell yourself that you're the best street-crosser in the world, and do it!"

There's more good advice in this than Myra realized, because experiencing the energy of your legs is the foundation for so many of the components of your self-development, including your BodyVoice.

Self-Sufficiency—Lower Abdomen

The lower torso is the location of what I call the Life Energy Center, an energetic focal point located about two to four fingers' width below your navel and about two to four fingers' depth inside your body. This energy center has been recognized and honored by many cultures, ancient and modern, around the globe. In Japan, it is called *Hara*, in the Middle East, *Kath*, and in China, *tan tien*. It is the source of the Samurai's *chi* energy still used in Karate and *t'ai chi ch'uan*. This center is experienced as a sense of being and knowing—beyond the mind. Its energy can be felt as a fullness that becomes an intimate sense of personal completeness and self-sufficiency. Years before I knew any of the traditions about this center, I thought of it as my Warm Button, and knew how necessary the experience of its body presence was for my voice. When I was in contact with this energy, I sounded good, full of aliveness. When I wasn't, not only did my voice suffer, but so did my sense of adequacy as well.

If the Life Energy Center is blocked by tension, emotional turmoil, or lack of vitality, you can experience a sense of deficiency or incompleteness, a worrisome feeling that no matter what you do, or how well you do it, or how sure of yourself you ought to be, there's something that's not right. This can come out as a feeling of inadequacy with no relation to your actual abilities. Roger, a jazz saxophonist who practiced up a storm, impressed every friend who dropped by his apartment with his lightning-fast fingering and wailing sound, but somehow he could never bring himself to join a band or perform. Whenever he sat in on a jam session, he would suddenly feel inadequate. He would even feel physically small, like a little boy towered over by huge adults—and Roger was six feet two inches tall. "I don't have what it takes," was the refrain in his mind. Roger's sense of deficiency began to ease as he worked with me on the development of his Life Energy Center.

I encourage the people I work with to learn how to focus their awareness on the Life Energy Center as a gateway to many other body energy experiences. Everyone experiences this center differently. It could feel like a bean sprout, a wave, or like sunshine. It could feel like anything—or like nothing. But as long as you check in on what you're feeling there, even noticing *nothing* is all right. The gentle but persistent monitoring can awaken that nothing into something that has the power to enhance your sense of individuality and personal presence.

Melissa was tall and slender, with a reserved but friendly air. She was in her early forties, happily married, and had raised four children. Her voice was thin-sounding and locked in her throat, and it had caused her problems as a community theater actress. When she started with me, she felt nothing of these energies and couldn't see how she ever would. I encouraged her to begin paying attention to her Life Energy Center as she Body Breathed and relaxed. With her permission, I want to share with you the following excerpts from her diary which show her development:

December 5. I've begun, as Joan suggested, focusing my awareness on my lower torso. "Just say hello to it," she said. Well, hello! It's been a week or so, and I don't feel much of anything there. It feels empty, like a concave black bowl. If this is my source of feelings of self-sufficiency, I'm sunk!

January 13. I felt something there today, but not very much. Joan was excited, said it was the first step. I was kind of dour about it. "Are you sure?" I asked her. "All I feel is this sensation of mild pressure—like a black hockey puck." She said not to judge whatever images come to mind. I don't get it.

February 13. I blushed with Joan today. I don't really know why. I smiled as I felt my whole body was blushing. My feelings are starting to change. Today, while I went through the De-Stresser Technique, then the Body Breathing, I felt . . . well, energy is a good word. A flicker of energy with a wonderful quality to it. I could feel myself calming down, filling with a new, but welcome, sense of security and strength and rightness. "Any specific feelings in your Center?" Joan asked. "Yes," I said. "It feels like an alive, green sprout." Like a seed coming to life, pushing its tendril up through the soil, fresh and alive.

April 9. Remarkable night! It's 2 A.M., and I'm writing this before I go to sleep—if I can sleep. I went out to the movies with Tim, saw two of my favorites, splurged on popcorn. We had a ball—must have been a premonition. On the walk home, I suddenly became aware of an emerging sensation in my lower torso. It was subtle, but sure—so wonderful I was astonished. Is this what Joan has been talking about? No wonder! It just amazes me how the feeling has such a full quality to it: I felt as if I, myself, my personal identity, was a living, palpable presence, not just a concept. It was ennobling, invigorating, centering . . . words can't fully describe it. I grabbed Tim's arm and laughed excitedly, "We've got to find a phone. I've got to tell Joan. I want to share this with her." Tim laughed and restrained me, "But it's after midnight. It'll wait to morning." And right now, as I continue to feel it and savor it, I know it will!

From that time on, her voice was able to stay open much more of the time, and her sound was able to reach a richness and depth she hadn't thought possible.

Will Power—Solar Plexus

The solar plexus is the energy center of your experience of will power and determination. The energy of this center has an unmistakable quality—a cool, precise knowledge of your ability to carry things through. When this energy is active in your life, you can feel empowered by a sense that you *can* do the things you set out to accomplish, that obstacles are challenges, that resources and solutions will be found, opportunities will materialize, and projects come to fruition as you keep moving onward to the attainment of your goals. The quality of a clear, firm, directed will can be communicated powerfully by the sound of your voice. Think of *Star Trek*'s Captain Kirk. When he asks Scottie for Warp 9 or for Bones to do the impossible, there's seldom an argument, because they can feel the will behind his determination to save his ship and crew at all costs. You can sense this quality in the many careers of Beverly Sills— opera singer, manager of the New York City Opera, TV commentator, wife, and mother. "I have another career in me," she said in a magazine interview, "and I'm sure it will show itself."[1] This is an example of someone who demonstrates magnificently: *I can*.

Without this internal solidity, you can fall prey to the feeling that you can't accomplish what you want, that obstacles block your growth, that life holds out no satisfying options or possibilities. At crucial junctures in your career and life plans, you may be enervated by an unjustified certainty of defeat. As you try to take action, the words "I can't do this" flash through your mind, and in your solar plexus area you have a sense of collapse and emptiness.

Brenda was a conscientious administrator in the health care field who, because of a lack of energy in this center, was very susceptible to whatever cynical attitudes circulated in her agency. She was a short, stocky brunette, with sensitive eyes, whose personality was inclined to enthusiasm. But on her job, she was often despondent.

"People just grouse, blow off steam," she said, "but I found I couldn't maintain a positive outlook. I'd hear someone grumble, 'They'll never give our project enough of a budget to do it right,' and I could feel the energy draining out of me. My body was like a sieve. I could feel my throat close up, and my voice fade. I started to think, 'Nothing will go right. Nothing will be there when I need it. No effort's worth it. Even if I achieve something, so what? There's never any gold at the end of the rainbow.'"

She found that focusing on her solar plexus when she was Body Breathing and monitoring her physical sensations during these negative situations helped her focus and amplify the "I can" sense in

[1] Katrine Ames, "Beverly in Bloom," *Savvy* (May 1987), p. 85.

her body, and soon she was much better at experiencing the positive feeling that directly related to her realistic capacity to act well in the midst of her professional pressure cooker.

"My body's not like a sieve anymore," she told me, "but like a strong vessel that holds a precious, calm Yes. I'm less bothered by other people's cynicism and I *know* I can get things done."

Her voice reflected her reclaimed ability.

Love and Compassion—Heart

In the performing arts, we can respond to all sorts of voices as long as they vividly communicate passion, humor, and individuality. Audiences are delighted with Humphrey Bogart's froggy cover-up of his vulnerability, James Cagney's seething toughness, or the childlike whoops of Goldie Hawn's zaniness, or Bea Arthur's distinct "Maude" and "Golden Girl" baritone.

I have a friend who's a storyteller for children, and her every "Once upon a time" always draws you in. She has worked mostly in radio, so her voice has become a garden of many sounds that keeps her listeners—young and old alike—enraptured.

The ability to express heartfelt emotions can begin with relaxation and Body Breathing to get release from the stressful feelings and muscular tensions that block emotion. But to go further, it means opening up to the deeper energies of the heart. If your chest is blocked by protective holding and shallow breathing, it doesn't just constrict your throat and vocal sound. It means the heartfelt emotions that can be reflected in the sound of your voice will be blocked, and so will the full texture of your loving and compassionate nature.

The heart cannot express itself if it's guarded, afraid, or closed. Randy, a dispassionate intellectual type, was surprised that his voice did not communicate the emotions he felt. We did a little test with a tape cassette. I asked Randy to talk about something that outraged him. He thought a moment, then told me the story of a colleague of his with whom he'd fought over the authorship of a theoretical paper.

When I stopped the cassette, he said, "That one stills burns me up. I'll bet I sounded mad."

I gently shook my head. "Your inflection sounded more like a question mark."

"I didn't mean it that way," he insisted, "and I'm sure it didn't sound that way."

"Let's listen," I said. I played back his story, and Randy became puzzled and quiet.

"How could I sound so flat and lifeless when I felt so angry inside?" he asked.

"You felt only a trickle of what's really bottled up in you emotionally. Your emotions are filtered and edited up here," I said, indicating his head. "If you'd been able to feel your anger completely, you would have experienced it strongly throughout your body. And *then* you would have heard it in the sound of your voice."

Andrew was a brilliant person with a lot of instinctual openness in his Life Energy Center, yet his heart energy was very repressed. With his thinning hair and weathered, scowling face, he looked the part of a hard-driving management consultant with no doubts about his abilities to handle the toughest contracts. But he had a rigid chest, and his voice had a hard edge on it.

When he began the exercises with me, he didn't like the idea of opening up his heart at all.

"Why bother?" he said with a scoffing shrug.

"To develop a better voice," I said, "you need to feel more."

Andrew's eyebrow went up. His eyes were cold.

"Why should I feel?" he replied in that cold voice of his. "I don't need a heart. I just want to get on with my life. What are feelings good for anyway? They just get in the way."

But as his work with me continued, Andrew learned a lot about a more emotionally receptive attitude in spite of himself. The exercises began to release his chest and his heart began to open. He found that a sly, truly engaging humor peeked out of the cracks in his armor, and this brought many interesting changes in his voice—more color, more humanness.

"I think you're beginning to see that you're sounding a lot better," I told him.

"Just so I don't sound like Mr. Soft Heart."

"No danger of that. But don't you also see how this is helping you to feel better, too?" I asked.

Andrew scowled. "I have to admit I do. I see that there *is* a way I might be able to express more of myself, more of what I deeply feel—in my own way."

On the other hand, there are many people who open their heart energies without the support of their Life Energy Center. They become vulnerable without a strong sense of self-sufficiency and a lot of times they get hurt. Teresa was a young actress working as an assistant buyer for a clothing wholesaler. Insecure, but very sensitive and compassionate, she had too little objectivity about important matters of the heart. Whether in a relationship, or dealing with people at work, or coping with the distressing news of the day, she put her heart into the keeping of others, without caution or wisdom; she just gave, and suffered. Teresa and I talked about self-sufficiency and the Life Energy Center, but it was difficult for her to imagine becoming more sure of her own needs without losing her sensitivity and caring for other people.

"I think of *Gone With the Wind*," she told me, "and the dichotomy between Scarlett O'Hara who could always take care of herself, even if rather heartlessly at times, and Melanie Wilkes who was, as Rhett Butler says, 'all heart' without strength."

"There's a way you can be enough of both," I assured her, and we began to work.

Opening up the heart can be a long journey, requiring many life experiences and the compassionate support and wisdom of many guides along the way. You can start to get some sense of the road by using the Kenley Method techniques to put more energy into your heart and to encourage and enhance feeling. Body Breathing can have a healthy, activating influence on the heart. And the sound of your BodyVoice, vibrating through your entire body, can have a healing effect on your heart energies. Then you may see better how to be sensitive without feeling you'll be hurt. You can begin to have a heart big and strong enough to take in all of life's feelings, a heart that is willing to feel deeply.

Self-Expression—Throat

If your throat is blocked, it doesn't mean just your voice is blocked. It means some of your creative energy is blocked. In the self-development schools that address the subtle energies I've been discussing, it is said that if you open up this area, you'll find your creative expression is enhanced, whether you're a writer, doctor, or football player. Anyone who wants to experience an expansion of this kind should explore any blocks that might exist in the throat area. It's no surprise that some people get their best ideas while singing in the shower!

Keith was a playwright-screenwriter could only work out his dialogue by getting up from his typewriter and acting out the parts. "At first," he said, "I thought it was because hearing the words actually spoken out loud was the only way to know if the dialogue would flow—if it had plausible cadence, pacing, and so on. But after a while, I realized there was more to it. I wasn't writing dialogue and then testing it out loud. *I was creating it as I spoke.* Speaking from the core impulses of the characters activated my throat in a way that made the creativity flow. As I spoke with my BodyVoice, I could express each character more clearly, and their words would pour into my head. Then I'd rush to the typewriter to get it all down."

People who hold back their full expression are more likely to get tired throats, become hoarse, or feel fatigued from a long spell of talking. There are times I might not choose to talk all day long, but I can speak just as expressively at the end of the day as at the beginning. The reason is that I talk in a full, energetic, charge-discharge pattern. So the way I speak is a way of sustaining my energy rather than losing it. My BodyVoice reenergizes my body. People who contract their throats inhibit their physical as well as creative energy.

Clarity—Mind

The demands you place on your thinking, mental understanding, and intellectual abilities probably rank higher in your awareness than some of the other energies we've just discussed. After all, so much of your daily life involves considerations of the mind. Every day at work and at home, you are aware of the hundreds of problems you must solve, decisions you must make, facts you must keep straight. Information and options abound, and you probably know only too well that you have good days and bad days in the mind department, days you feel sharp and tuned in, days you feel burned out. You probably have experienced what it's like when your mind is clear and unworried, your thinking freed of conflict and confusion—and what it's like when you have a mental block, when you simply can't think or make decisions. And, if you reflect on it, you can probably recall what your voice is like on those good days and bad days. When your mind is calm, your voice articulates your thoughts clearly, and when your mind is in a rut, it's very difficult to communicate precisely, almost as if your mind were a badly tuned engine and your vocal expression running on less than all cylinders.

The mind is like a computer, with programs, files, and interconnections—better in some ways than any computer yet designed. The mind can create clarity, manipulate information, and access knowledge when working in a balanced harmony with the body. The heart and the Life Energy Center have their ways of "knowing" as well—not in the way the mind handles and collects information, but through an emotional and intuitive knowledge that reaches beyond academic or intellectual pursuits. When you can release the mental contractions that make thinking such an effort, you can begin to use so many other sources within you. You will also find that releasing the blocked energies of the mind can give great relief—a beautiful sense of peace. Imagine the abundant knowing of your Life Energy Center, the loving pulse of your heart, the creative expression of your throat, and the sparkling, peaceful clarity of your mind united in a free-flowing stream of energy that is reflected in your body, voice, and life.

"They invented the phrase 'burning the midnight oil' for me," said Gary, an advertising man in charge of administrative planning and budgeting for large campaigns. "I used to brainstorm, trying to get at all the data—remember everything, overlook nothing. A million details! I'd get locked into a mental rut, pressure building, tension off the scale. I couldn't eat or sleep. I'd be up all night trying to remember what I was sure I had forgotten—completely losing my grasp of the big picture.

"Finally, usually between two and three in the morning, the tension and frustration would become too much. 'I give up,' I'd say to myself. 'This time it's all over. I'm all washed up.' A great wave of resignation would wash over me. And immediately, as if released from a spell, my mind would come to life. Facts, figures, planning ideas, contacts, resources, precedents, schedules—all would come pouring into my mind, and I'd have my plan."

"Sounds exhausting," I said. "And like a big waste of your energy."

"You bet it was," he said. "But now, I'm learning how to avoid putting so much pressure on my mind while I shut down my body. Your body awareness and relaxation techniques—along with the Body Breathing—have really helped."

Gary's voice gained from the exercises, too. When he was in one of his mental ruts, he not only looked tense and on the edge, he sounded immensely strained. His co-workers became nervous and agitated just listening to him. He was communicating his sense of personal apocalypse. But once he had learned to restore a balance between his mind and body energies, his eyes took on new sparkle and life; his entire face became more expressive; and he spoke with a richness that truly reflected the wealth of his mind.

The Power of Body Awareness

You may be wondering, Why haven't I been cultivating this inner body awareness all along? If it's so important, why hasn't it been a natural evolution of your self-development?

In most cultures today, this kind of inner awareness is not considered as part of family life nor addressed in school. Modern life seems designed in a way that keeps your body too tense to allow the expression and experience of these more refined physical energies. As a result, many people tend to function from their intellects at the expense of their body aliveness. Kurtz and Prestera point out:

> As we are all well aware, in our contemporary culture, the mind is very highly trained and placed in control of the lower, instinctual belly mind [lower torso energies] . . .

> As long as we continue to overeducate with mind structures, our vitality will suffer[2]

All too often, people are content with a limited sensory life experience, as if a healthy body is simply a well-oiled, smoothly running machine. Richer body sensory experiences are considered exceptional, and are expected only in exceptional moments. Think of when you were moved by a beautiful painting or symphony, or the birth of a baby, or falling in love. Falling in love can be a supreme body experience, when you feel strength, power, completion, and forgive yourself for any deficiencies in image or worth. It can feel like a powerful surging and awakening in a very physical way, like sap flowing in a tree in the spring, like a waterfall released from winter ice. You might have a sense of rebirth, rejuvenation. The scales fall from your eyes, the world looks fresh, and you feel, feel, feel, in a body that seems so fabulously alive.

Kurtz and Prestera confirm this:

> When we are able to align ourselves physically and emotionally, we open a channel to receive this energy and, in doing so, we

[2] Ron Kurtz and Hector Prestera, M.D., *The Body Reveals* (New York: Harper and Row, 1976), pp. 67–68.

become awakened on a level hardly to be compared with ordinary consciousness. This heightened consciousness is not simply intellectual; it involves our very tissues.[3]

Nathan and Sarah loved driving cross-country on their vacations, seeing natural wonders, enjoying the open road.

"There was an experience we had," he told me, "that always impressed me and made me want to understand more about myself."

Nathan told me that they had decided, as many travelers are advised, to cross the deserts of the Great Basin at night to miss the furnace temperature of the summer day. So they did just that during a full moon. The desert was beautiful in a dreamlike way, and he and Sarah fell into a long conversation.

"There's something magical," he said, "about the kind of talks you have driving all night. The world seems open to new possibilities. You feel free. The car radio picks up stations from all over the continent. Barriers go down, and you really speak from your heart."

They had touched on many things in their lives, it seemed. They talked about their relationship and worked out many facets of it with more tenderness and insight than they had thought possible. They went over their career decisions, the other people in their lives, their responsibilities, their freedoms.

"I have never felt so in touch," he said. "My mind was clear, my heart full. I was filled with life and determination. When dawn came, like a line of fire over the desert hills, the feeling slowly receded. The magic of the night faded, the radio stations dimmed into static, and slowly we came back down to the feeling of another day. We wanted breakfast, coffee, and rest. But I vowed to myself that I would learn about how to feel that way more often—not just once every two years on a vacation, but every normal working day of my life."

"Well, you've come to the right place," I said. "You don't need a moonlight drive in the desert to get in touch with those core feelings. They are energetic qualities you can bring forth by learning to be aware of them in your body and your voice."

In fact, paying attention to body sensations is the key for contacting and *feeling* these energies directly as inherent colors of aliveness in your life and voice. The healthy flow of these energies is

[3]*The Body Reveals*, p. 18.

also encouraged by Body Breathing and by developing the resonance of your BodyVoice. You don't have to do anything extraordinary to contact them. The first step is just to say hello to various
parts of yourself. Ask what's going on in there. Frequently during
the day, pose these kind of questions to yourself:

What do I feel throughout my body?

How can I precisely describe the energies of my legs, lower torso, solar
plexus, heart, throat, and mind in terms of sensations or images?

When I am aware of my body energies, how does it affect the way I
behave?

What does my voice feel and sound like when I'm in touch with these
energies?

Time will make you more familiar with details and you'll start to
notice a new level of personal energetic experience in your body and
in your voice.

Dean, a corporate counsel who needed help with hoarseness,
couldn't quite grasp what I meant by levels of personal body energies. But one day, after a session with me, while we were making
small talk before he went back to the office, he was telling me how he
and his wife Nikki were finally going to do some remodeling on their
beloved house. Suddenly, he became eloquent as he reminisced
about the history of their home.

"When we first found the place," he said, "it was just an exterior
to us. We sat in the car, in front of the For Sale sign, looking at the
porch and windows and white paneling, wondering what it was like
inside. Then we went on a tour with the real estate agent and saw all
the rooms—the fireplace, the den, the master bedroom with its
amazing closets, the kitchen with its breakfast nook, and so on—
and we began to get excited about its aesthetic and practical possibilities. Well, we bought it, and we moved in."

As I grew more interested, Dean reflected further. "We really
made that house into our home. Of course," he laughed, "we learned
all about its quirks and faults. We worked on plumbing, and the tree
roots that buckled the swimming pool deck, and we found out how
the mulberry tree dropped thousands of catkins every spring. We
knew just where the roof tended to leak. And we patiently fixed it
up."

"Quite a project," I said.

"Yes, but it was a labor of love. And now, we feel so much a part of our home. We know all the moods of the house, how the rooms look in each season. 'There's a certain slant of light on winter after-noons'—Emily Dickinson, right? I know the sound of the rain as we're lying in bed in the morning, the buzz of the refrigerator in the kitchen when I go for a glass of water in the middle of the night. I know how the backyard looks when the fog descends, how the flowers fill the back door with color on a spring day. I know the way the dining room looks in candlelight, and how the stereo sounds with the new carpeting, and how cozy the den is when we're watching TV. Definitely a home now."

I was absolutely amazed at this evocation of complex, intimate sensory experiences, and said, "Dean, I think you would do well to explore your body with the same poetic sensitivity you've expressed about your house."

If you can think about sensing your body energies in the spirit of Dean's loving relationship with his house, you'll have taken a big step toward understanding how to focus your awareness on the sensory life of your body. At first, your body may only be an exterior to you. You know what your face looks like in the mirror, and how you look in different clothes—when you're all dressed up for a night on the town or in old togs for just loafing around. Then, you begin to learn what's *inside*. Initially, it's the most easily accessible feelings, sensations, and energies that you become aware of and experience. You know what tension your muscles carry, your normal aches and pains, your sense of fullness or emptiness. You know things about how you get tired, or anxious—and *where* you do: the crick in your neck when you've done too much paperwork, the sweaty palms when you have a confrontation, the headache you get from red wine, the sore throat when you've burned the candle at both ends. The rest is ignored as long as it functions.

But as you develop a deeper body awareness, you can begin to experience a more intimate level of physical sensation and feel even more at home with your body, just as Dean and Nikki learned about the subtle delights of living in their house. Your body also has its seasons, its moods, its sunlight and shadow. You can deepen your emotional experiences—such as feelings of strength, confidence, and love—so that they can be felt at a level of experience that touches your refined body energies.

I'm sure you're already aware that there are times when you have a sense of lightness, of mobility, of abounding richness, and other times when you feel heaviness, rigidity, or muffled and muzzy, or lik a lump of clay. You know the days your body sings, the days it complains. You live, in fact, in an unending variety of emotional states and body sensations; dozing off on a sunny weekend afternoon, sluggishness on a rainy day when you're trapped inside, pangs of nostalgia for people and places gone by, the fire of love or ambition, the glow of participating in times of excitement and adventures, the heaviness of sorrow or worry on your heart. You might experience exhilaration as cartwheels in your legs urging you to sprint over the next hill, or fatigue as if you're wrapped in gauze like a mummy. You might have times you feel cleansed, refurbished, and renewed, times you feel young and full of freshness, and times you feel withered and dry. As you come to know yourself on this more refined, more intimate level of body awareness, you can be more in tune with all aspects of your life, and you can learn to release more of your personal expressiveness into the sound of your BodyVoice.

Trying Softer

Many times people yearn to be in contact with these finer qualities in their lives without knowing how to go about it. Because society or the people around them talk about having certain emotions—such as a mother's love, a teacher's compassion, a friend's trust—people automatically assume they understand and know these qualities, whether or not they actually feel them as completely as they can potentially be experienced. You can believe you have a certain emotion, like love, and then take whatever you feel for the reality of the emotion.

Any sincere quest toward knowing more about yourself and your inner life can be valuable. In fact, it is possible for you, through your own efforts and self-discipline, courage, and tenacity, to realize more contact with the qualities you desire. You know what doors you want to open and may even have a good idea of what's behind those doors. Developing a body energy focus can be like finding the key to some of those locks. As you work with this book, I would also encourage you to investigate workshops, seminars, and private teachers who can facilitate your adventure into further self-exploration.[4]

[4]For an introduction to the work of Dr. Almaas, see *Essence: The Diamond Approach to Inner Realization*, (York Beach, Maine: Samuel Weiser, Inc., 1986), and *Diamond Heart* (Berkeley, Cal.: Diamond Books, 1987).

People try too hard sometimes, and that's why I often repeat, "Try softer." Trying too hard turns into mental and physical effort, and the body energies become blocked. You may be familiar with many of the patterns that emerge:

> People who force themselves to take on challenges and new experiences while trembling inside and feeling they might stumble at any moment;

> People who stay with a small circle of friends, environments, and ideas where they can feel pretty much ok, without the inner sureness that allows for real exploration and risk-taking;

> People who struggle with grim determination toward their goals, needing constant encouragement from others, but never feeling the assurance of their own will power;

> People who make loving, caring gestures without experiencing any heartfelt emotions;

> People who are willing to accept the way they express themselves and work through ideas without experiencing the inner fire of creativity or the light of mental clarity.

As you learn to "try softer," remember that your personality has its own unique strengths and weaknesses. Just because you haven't been consciously focusing on your body sensations, don't assume that all your inner energies are unavailable to you. Maybe you have a sensitive, caring heart, but need to develop the self-sufficiency that comes from your Life Energy Center. Or you may have a lot of will power, but find your determination thwarted by the kind of creativity blocks and confused thinking associated with contractions in the throat and mind centers. Enjoy the discovery of your own individuality, and you'll eventually identify where your body energies are blocked—and where they are flowing. Then you'll have a sense of what course your self-development should take, and be able to choose more clearly your important first steps toward enhancing the full energetic life of your body and your voice.

Part 2

The Kenley Method Techniques

Introduction

Relax! That's the way to begin with the Kenley Method. Easy does it, take your time, and enjoy each step.

First, let's look at some tips for using this method. At each step, keep in mind that relaxation and awareness of your body are the keys.

Everyone knows that practice makes perfect. It is also true in this method. But practice does not mean over-exertion or conducting an endurance contest. Be *curious* about discovering all facets of what will happen to your body and your voice, and be interested in the dynamics of the process rather than judgmental or overly results oriented. Be patient and you'll actually go faster.

It is important to be sure you have a good understanding of each step before you go on to the next. Then, by following the suggestions in each chapter and using your own judgment and knowledge of yourself, you'll be able to gently, comfortably, sensibly integrate the exercises into your daily life.

Some of the techniques you will want to practice in a quiet, secluded place once or twice a day. Others, like the BodyVoice relaxation exercises and the Body Breathing, will become a part of the rhythm of your daily activities.

Some Helpful Suggestions

To be prepared for each part of the exercises, it will help to have the following:

Loose clothing to wear when you practice the exercises. Constricting belts or tight pants will inhibit your relaxation and breathing. In general, I encourage people never to wear any clothes that restrict healthy breathing.

A beeper watch. This can be a great help in reminding you throughout the day to do the De-Stresser Technique once an hour.

An audio cassette player with earphones. I recommend this over any other kind of tape recorder, because of the accuracy you will want when listening to the sound of your voice. Earphones can provide almost studio quality reproduction, and you'll hear more of your good vocal qualities, as well as those that need work.

Stick-em notes and adhesive colored dots. These will be useful to post as constant daily reminders to Body Breathe.

Completed copies of your BodyVoice Self-Evaluation questionnaire, BodyVoice Evaluation questionnaires, and Kenley Method Proficiency Guide and Evaluation Chart. These will be helpful as references for you as you learn to relax, increase your awareness of body sensations, and make progress toward your goal of becoming a dynamic, effective communicator.

Where and How to Practice the Exercises

In each of the following chapters, you will find clear instructions on how to practice each step, with illustrations to aid you. If you follow the instructions, referring to the book as much as you need to, your *body* will learn these exercises and make them a natural part of your everyday life.

How Long to Work with the Kenley Method

You're probably wondering how long you will have to work with these exercises before you see significant results. The most important thing to keep in mind is that *preparation is 75 percent of the effectiveness of the techniques.*

You may be tempted by impatience to hurry through the exercises and skip your vocal warm-ups so that you can start right in Body Speaking and dazzle the world with your new voice. But the real change in your communication skills will come from making the relaxation exercises, Body Breathing, and body awareness a natural part of your life. Don't forget the important principles of the body-mind-emotion unity on which these exercises are based. Each exercise not only helps you develop your vocal expressiveness and power, but also enhances your health and well-being. The techniques will feel relaxing, soothing, *energizing*. After all, it's not possible for a beautiful voice to come from a nervous, rigid body.

Generally, you should have a good understanding of the exercises and a fuller experience of your voice within six weeks. This progress should encourage you to deepen your understanding of the BodyVoice concept, and to continue until the techniques are an integral part of your life. True mastery, as in other life pursuits, comes from a permanent commitment to self-exploration and excellence.

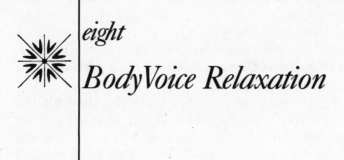

eight

BodyVoice Relaxation

The first step in the Kenley Method exercises is to learn a very specific way of achieving a calm yet alive state of mind-body relaxation—quickly and effectively. Before you learn to Body Breathe, before you learn to make a single Body Sound, you want to be able to let go of stressful feelings and start releasing tension-bound muscles. To release your BodyVoice with the help of this method, you must first lay the foundation by relaxing physically and emotionally.

I will show you two sets of exercises to help you achieve a more relaxed body and a clearer state of mind:

The De-Stresser Technique
Exercises to further relax the Triangle of Tension formed by your head, neck, and shoulders

The De-Stresser Technique

The combination of exercises I call De-Stresser Technique will help you become more sensitive to your body and allow you to relax quickly whenever you start to feel stressed, wherever you are.

Gaining special sensitivity to your body is very important in achieving the ability to relax. Review what occurs in your body when you feel stressed, threatened, or nervous:

144

What happens to your breathing?

Do your shoulders tense or does your back ache?

How about your heartbeat?

Does your voice get higher or tighter?

Do you find your stomach contracting?

Does your gut go into a turmoil?

Does your mind go blank?

As you become more body oriented, you will become more aware of your specific body-emotion reactions—and you'll begin to appreciate how important this technique is for you. After all, your head, heart, stomach, and gut, along with breathing irregularities and muscle contractions, are the target places and responses that cause you mental and physical suffering.

It's critical to learn how to notice your tension when you are under stress. Tension can be like a thief who's ravaged your house while you've been asleep. I want you to sound the alarm for yourself before this insidious thief even reaches your front door—before your negative body energies have done their worst with you. That's why I want you to begin with a de-stressing, relaxing, tuning-into-your-body exercise.

The De-Stresser Technique is an efficient emotional detoxifier. It will help you to put aside wandering thoughts and sense your body more deeply. You will slow down your breathing and sense your arms and legs in a special way.

I will take you through the De-Stresser Technique in five stages:

Sensing your body—a "before" inventory

Focusing on your arms and legs

Holding your breath

Combining Steps 1, 2, and 3

Follow-up—an "after" inventory

Step 1: Sensing Your Body

- Lie horizontally, eyes closed, on the floor or on a firm bed, whichever is more comfortable for you. If your back hurts when you lie flat, do the exercise with your knees bent.
- Begin by taking an inventory of how you are experiencing your body (see figure 1). Ask yourself the following types of questions:

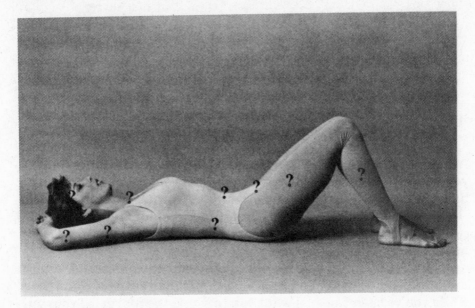

Figure 1. Personal Inventory of Body Sensations

What can you sense in your body at this moment?
What's happening in your gut?
Is your stomach tight or relaxed?
What sensations are in your chest?
What do you feel in your throat?
Is your brain chattering?

Your answers will help you get a sense of your physical and emotional state *before* you begin your relaxation. In Step 5 you will take another body-mind-emotion inventory *after* doing the relaxation exercises.

Get used to mentally exploring your body this way, gently focusing your attention on different areas, receptive to whatever sensations you may become aware of. Don't worry about what you sense—or don't sense. At this stage, the important thing is the act of focusing your attention. All living things love attention: Your body is no exception.

Step 2: Focusing on Your Arms and Legs

Your arms and legs are the emotionally neutral parts of your body. When you're under stress, they remain on the sidelines while fear, anger, anxiety, and conflicts wage war in your mind, throat, chest, stomach, and gut. By focusing your attention on your arms and legs, you begin the process of releasing negative energy from your body's stress reactions and from tension-generating emotions, and you start to calm down.

- Use your hands to lightly slap each arm and each leg a few times—up one side and down the other, to heighten your sensations.
- Sense your arms and legs now. To begin with, just try to see if you can get a basic awareness of them:

> Can you sense if they feel light or heavy? Are they resting lightly on the floor like pieces of wood floating in water? Or are they feeling heavy as if they were water-logged?
> Check your perception of their width and length. Do they feel long or short? Can you sense the changes in shape and dimension of your arms from shoulder to biceps to elbow to forearm to wrist to hands? Focus on your thighs, knees, calves, ankles, and feet in the same way.

- Let's get even more body specific. When you sense your arms internally, can you feel:

> Your bones, blood, muscles and energy?
> Any density and dimension?
> Any pulsing or tingling?

- Next, focus on your legs, and go through the same questions.
- Then, increase your mental attention on your arms and legs by saying, not out loud, but silently and slowly with your mind:

> "A-r-m-s,   a-r-m-s,   l-e-g-s,   l-e-g-s."

- You may want to focus on just one arm at a time, and then one leg; or both arms, then both legs. Do what's comfortable—customize the exercise so it works for you.
- Put your mental and physical attention on your arms and legs for a couple of minutes while closing your eyes and breathing quietly.

Take your time with this. Let awareness of your arms and legs override other body sensations (see figure 2)—it's a key part of this technique).

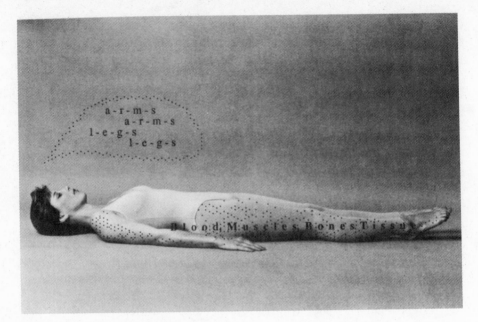

Figure 2. Sensing Arms & Legs

Step 3: Holding Your Breath

- Take a normal breath—not a big one—and exhale about half way, finding a place that feels good to you.
- Hold your breath with your lungs partially empty for as long as it's comfortable.
- Then exhale any air that remains and breathe normally.

If you felt like gasping, you're trying to hold your breath too long. Don't make this a breath-holding contest. Try holding your breath with a partial exhalation a few more times. The point is to find a level and duration that's comfortable for you. This breathing technique can calm you when you're overcharged and release energy when you're withdrawn or shut down.

Step 4: Combine Steps 1, 2, 3

- Close your eyes, take a mind-body inventory.
- Monitor your arms and legs, mentally and physically, as you hold your breath with your lungs partially empty.
- Try this at least five times in succession.

Step 5: Follow-Up

After completing Steps 1 through 4, take another inventory of your body sensations. Ask yourself:

- How do I feel now?
- Are my arms and legs heavier or lighter than before?
- Is my mind quieter? clearer?
- Have the feelings or sensations in my gut, stomach, and chest changed?

Compare this "after" inventory with the "before" inventory you took of yourself in Step 1. In doing so, you may realize that you could relax even further. So do the full exercise, Steps 1 through 5, again. If you find in your "before" inventory of body sensations that you're extremely nervous or stressed, you may need to sense your limbs and hold your breath ten, twenty, or thirty times. Be your own judge. Be your own body detective. Do the exercise as many times as you need to fully relax.

Once you've become familiar with the technique, go directly to Step 4 and then finish with Step 5.

If you don't feel energized enough to continue your activities, you can activate more energy with this sequence:

- Take three short doggie pants and one long exhalation.
- Repeat this breathing pattern several times.
- Stop and check how you feel. This should help re-energize you.

This quick exercise can be used any time during the day to get more movement and aliveness in your body.

When and Where to Use the De-Stresser Technique

The best position to practice this exercise is lying on your back with your eyes closed. Later on, you'll find you can go through the same routine (with your eyes open!) while driving, walking, fixing dinner, or watching television—and get just as effective results.

You should do the De-Stresser Technique once an hour throughout the day. Use your beeper watch or other kinds of reminders to help you remember.

If you become used to doing it regularly, when you are not under any particular stress, you'll find it will work much better when you really need it: before an important speech, a critical meeting, or a touchy interview.

The De-Stresser Technique should be part of your preparation in doing all of the exercises in the Kenley Method. Always start with this exercise before you go on to your Body Breathing or producing Body Sounds. No one thing will help improve your communication skills as much as learning to begin everything you do from a state of mind-body-emotion relaxation—calm, alert, ready for action.

Special De-Stressing Tips

Consider this investigation a pleasurabale way of making more contact with your body. However, if you tend to be a mental type of person, it might create some temporary discomfort for you to be more in touch with your body sensations. The goal here is for you to experience your body as both peaceful and alive, to be what can be called "in residence" in your body. Eventually, you will be able to feel more of *yourself* by sensing more of your *body*.

Since you can also do this exercise without lying down or closing your eyes, you can easily explore what it's like to "stop the world" at any time—to get away from your busy, chattering mind by focusing inside your body. This serves to anchor your body just like a ship is anchored in the water, so you aren't adrift in mental confusion. As you become more conscious of your arms and legs in your daily life, you'll become more aware of what you're actually *doing* from moment to moment, and you'll also start to notice how you're really breathing, speaking, and feeling.

Always begin the exercise with a sense of *curiosity* about what you're going to experience. After all, you are never exactly the same person you were a minute ago or an hour ago. Approaching this technique with a fresh sense of self-discovery will add greatly to its effectiveness.

As you learn to feel at ease in every part of your body, you are reminded that nothing should be tense, nothing held tight. In fact, after you've practiced this exercise for a couple of weeks, you can begin to focus awareness on your own favorite place for contracting and holding in tension. When you do the focusing on your arms and legs while holding your breath, say silently to yourself:

"A-r-m-s, l-e-g-s, n-e-c-k.
"A-r-m-s, l-e-g-s, l-o-w-e-r b-a-c-k."

Direct your awareness where it will do you the most good.

Now let's go on to some even more specific ways to relax your shoulders, your neck, your chin, and your face.

Releasing Your Triangle of Tension

Releasing your Triangle of Tension (see figure 3) is designed to help you let go of hidden tensions in your shoulders, neck, and head that must be released for your BodyVoice to develop.

There are four parts to this release:

Tension release
Yawning
Releasing your jaw and chin
Looking dough-faced

Step 1: Tension Release

- Lie flat, or with your knees bent, and explore your skull, face, jaw, chin, neck, and shoulders with your fingers and hands.
- Find out where you have tightness and where you are more relaxed.
- Gently massage any areas that you find are rigid or tender.
- Encourage yourself to "try softer," not harder.

Step 2: Yawning

- Yawn—a big, impolite yawn.
- Do you feel what happens inside your throat?
- Your vocal cords should seem wider, as if they were a parachute puffing open, right at the height of the yawn (see figure 4).
- Picture that your vocal cords are parallel and very loose; imagine that the space between them is as wide as the space between your ear lobes.
- Don't attempt to be polite and controlled; you should go for a full, let-it-all-out yawn. And yawn any time you want to recapture that open-throat sensation. Try to carry a sense memory of this feeling with you.

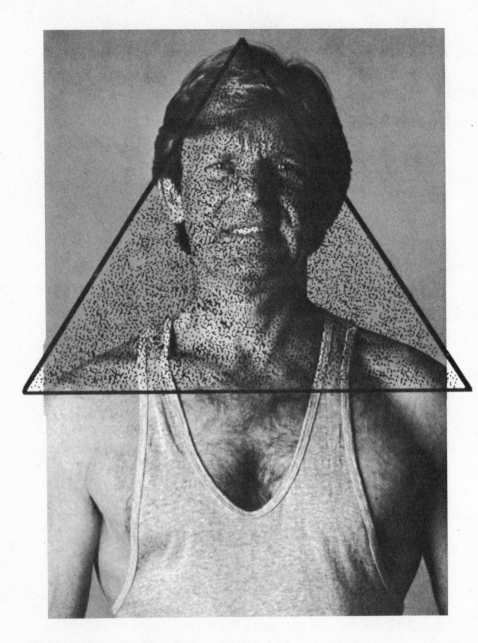

Figure 3. Triangle of Tension

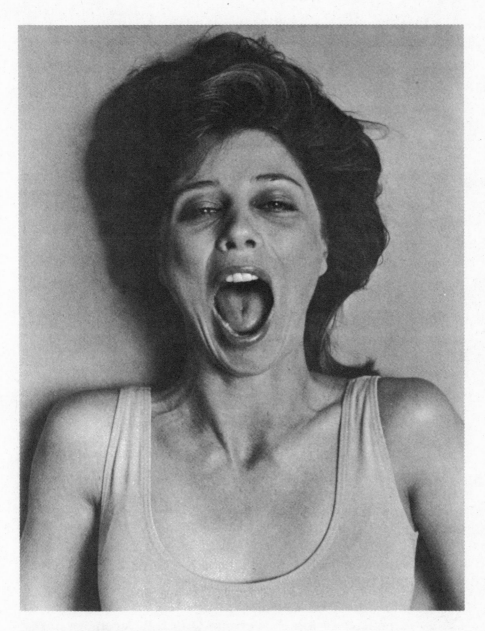

Figure 4. Yawning to Open the Throat

Step 3: Relaxing Your Jaw and Chin

A tight jaw and chin will give you a tight-sounding voice, so it's important to relax them.

- Open your mouth slightly.
- Take the palm of your hand and place it gently on your chin. Let the warmth of your palm soften your muscles and tissues so that your chin melts toward the back of your head (not down toward your throat). If you are doing this correctly, you should feel as though you have protruding front teeth (see figure 5).
- Observe how releasing your chin and jaw will relax your neck. If you feel any pressure on your throat, it means you've pulled your chin back instead of releasing it.
- Try to keep this position and remember this feeling after you've taken your palm away.

Step 4: Looking Dough-Faced

To cap off your relaxation, your expression should look like a dough-faced character—as if all your facial muscles have turned to mush (see figure 6).

- Take your left hand and place it gently on your left cheek, and put your right hand on your right cheek.
- Let your face melt under the warmth of your hands.
- Notice whether your shoulders, your neck, your jaw, and your face feel softer and more relaxed.

You want to become an expert at monitoring your own tension. Try to feel as if your face, neck, shoulders, and torso above your navel are made of jello.

Monitoring your shoulders, neck, chin, jaw, and face is an integral sequential step in practicing this technique, but it can be used by itself throughout the day as needed.

BodyVoice Relaxation Exercises—Quick Reference Chart

The De-Stresser Technique

- Lie down or sit comfortably and sense your body and emotional state.
- Exhale partially and hold your breath while you sense your arms and

Figure 5. Jaw and Chin Release

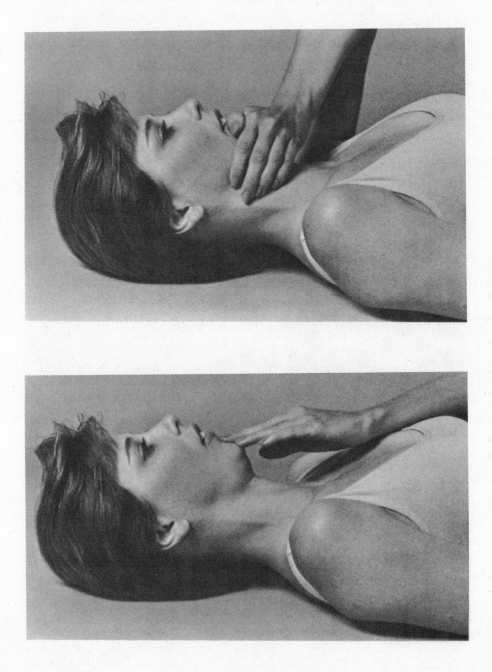

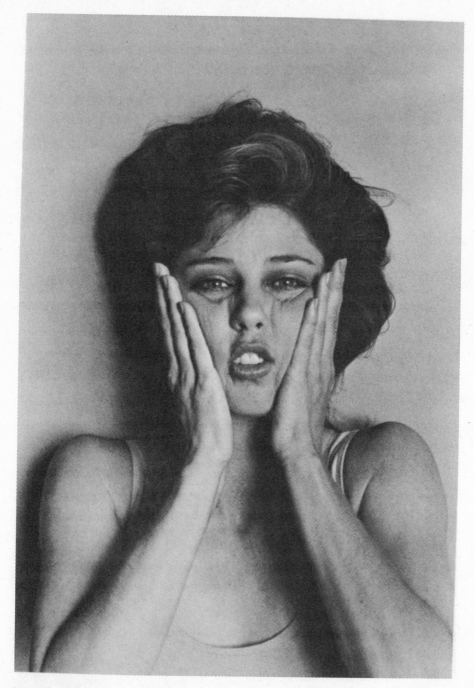

Figure 6. Facial Relaxation

legs internally; silently repeat A-R-M-S, A-R-M-S, L-E-G-S, L-E-G-S, in your mind.
- Then exhale any air that may be left, inhale again, partially exhale, hold your breath, and focus again on your arms and legs.
- Do this at least five times—more if you need to.
- Recheck your body and emotional state.

Releasing Your Triangle of Tension

- Gently massage your skull, face, jaw, neck, and shoulders with your fingers.
- Yawn. Notice how your vocal cords stretch open and relax. Keep a yawn feeling in your throat.
- Open your mouth slightly. Lay the palm of your hand on your chin to release it back toward your ears. Use your hands on your cheeks to soften your face. Look dough-faced.

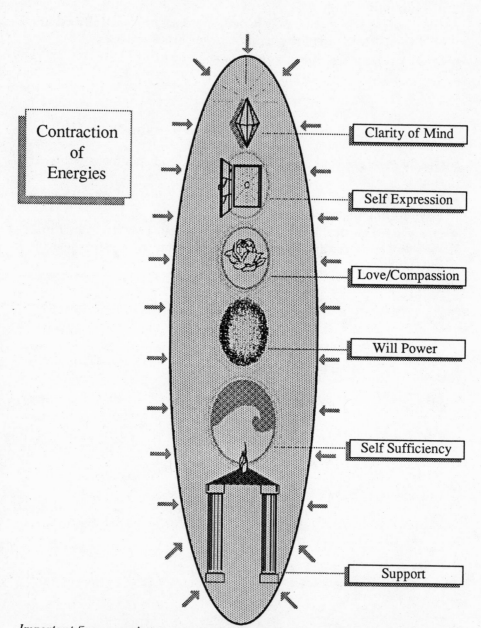

Contraction
of
Energies

Clarity of Mind

Self Expression

Love/Compassion

Will Power

Self Sufficiency

Support

Important finer energies operate throughout your body and can be experienced as emotional qualities associated with your legs, lower abdomen, solar plexus, heart, throat, and mind. When you are stressed, closed down, or feeling harsh about yourself, these energies contract, and your mental and physical well-being is diminished.

nine
Body Breathing Exercises

To learn to Body Breathe, begin by locating the muscles in the lowest part of your torso that move when you cough. I call them, collectively, your Body Breathing Muscle. To prepare for the Body Breathing exercises, use the De-Stresser and other relaxation techniques explained in Chapter 8 to get yourself into a relaxed state. Picture the whole top part of your body—face, neck, shoulders, and torso above your navel—as passive: imagine that it doesn't have to *do* anything. You'll soon experience your upper body as *receiving* the breath and sound that will seem to originate in your lower body (see figure 7).

The Body Breathing Muscle Movement

Refer to figure 8 as you follow these instructions:

- Lie down and put your hands on your lower torso below your navel.
- Simply cough gently.
- Feel the muscular movement with your hands.
- Lift your Body Breathing Muscle up and let it fall a few times to get the feel of it.

How to Body Breathe

- Breathe in with your mouth and let the inhalation lift your lower torso—the area *below* your navel.

159

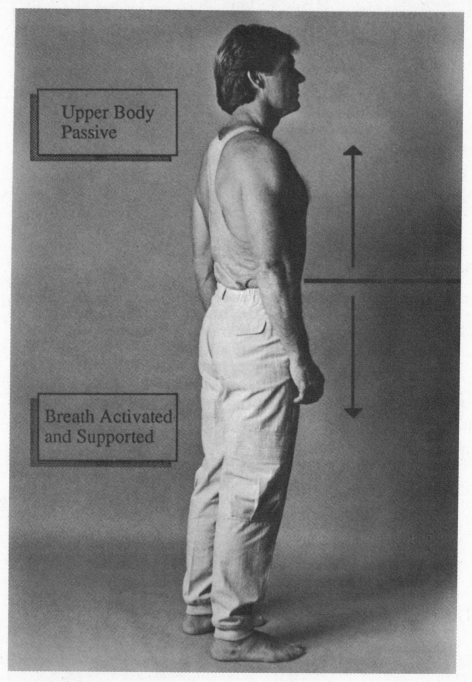

Figure 7. BodyVoice Breathing

Figure 8. Body Breathing

A. *Inhale, Expanding Body Breathing Muscle*

B. *Exhale, Releasing Body Breathing Muscle*

- Feel as if the air is going deeply into the very bottom of your body.
- Don't make any effort to lift the middle part of your torso where your diaphragm is located—it will respond naturally with some expansion to your Body Breathing Muscle movement.
- Your upper chest should have very little noticeable response to your inhalation.
- Exhale by slowly letting your Body Breathing Muscle fall in toward your spine, as it moves the wave of air up and out of your body.
- Try five easy Body Breaths; see how they feel.

Although many people are more concerned with the way they inhale, be aware that your exhalation is every bit as important. Visualize a wave of breath that is inhaled into your lower body and exhaled smoothly up through your torso and out through your yawning, relaxed throat and partially open mouth.

Use mouth breathing for these exercises and for all speaking in this method. When you are not talking, nose breathing is preferable, using your Body Breathing Muscle in the same way.

Now I want you to sit up *slowly* (if you're not used to this deep breathing, it might cause you to be somewhat light-headed), and see if you can Body Breathe while sitting in a chair.

- First of all, cough again to locate your Body Breathing Muscle.
- Body Breathe gently from your lower body.
- Notice, with one hand on your chest, whether your chest falls significantly when you exhale. It shouldn't. Your upper body is not supposed to be rigid, but softly *stable,* while you Body Breathe in the same way you learned lying down.
- Try five breaths.
- Then try to Body Breathe standing up.

If you find any difficulties breathing this way while you are sitting or standing, try it again lying down. It's sometimes easier to go through this exercise in a horizontal position.

When and Where to Body Breathe

You should begin to breathe this way *all* the time, wherever you are throughout the day. But since breathing is not something you usually think about, it's almost impossible to keep your attention on this task without some help.

I suggest you put written notes or some other kind of reminders where you live and work—in places where you'll be sure to see them as you go through your day. Colored adhesive dots or stick-em notes can be placed on your telephone, refrigerator, checkbook, car door, steering wheel, bathroom mirror, or wherever you know they'll catch your eye and remind you. People who bombard their environment with reminders to Body Breathe always become full-time Body Breathers faster than those who don't.

When you first learn to breathe using your lower torso muscles, the movement during your exercises should be exaggerated to get the feel of it. But throughout the day and as you eventually learn Body Speaking, a much smaller movement is appropriate.

As you practice, the *feeling* of Body Breathing will become a greater part of your body consciousness. The more you become aware of your Body Breathing and your newly emerging body energy, the easier it will be to develop your BodyVoice. If you like, you can spend the next few days working on your breathing or move ahead now to Body Sounds.

Body Breathing Exercises—Quick Reference Chart

- Lying down, cough to find your Body Breathing Muscle, which is in your lower torso below your navel.
- Take a deep Body Breath in through your mouth and let your inhalation lift your Body Breathing Muscle away from your spine.
- Let your exhalation gently flow up through your body, through a yawning throat and out a partly open mouth. Be sure your chin is softly released.
- As you exhale, your Body Breathing Muscle moves toward your spine.
- Try Body Breathing while sitting, then standing.
- Remember to put up breathing reminders, so you'll keep practicing your Body Breathing throughout the day.

ten

Producing Body Sounds

Now that you've learned how to practice relaxing your body and to Body Breathe from your lower torso, you're ready to learn how to release vocal sounds that feel like they originate from your lower body. The exercises in this chapter will show you how to experience a powerful resonant quality in your voice.

You will learn to produce Body Sounds in three stages:

The panting **UH** Body Sound

Producing **UH + OH, AH,** and **AY** Body Sounds

From panting groups to single sounds

The Panting UH Body Sound

To begin, lie down with your knees up, and go through your BodyVoice Relaxation and Body Breathing exercises if you haven't already done so.

Preparation for Body Sounds

- Put your little finger between your teeth at one side of your mouth, without biting down on your finger, to gauge the optimal space between your lips and teeth for your Body Sounds (figure 9).

Figure 9. Preparation for Sound—Correct Mouth Opening

- In that position, your hand will fall lightly on your cheek, and your other fingers or the side of your hand can still be checking to see whether your chin is remaining soft.
- If your mouth won't stay in that position when you remove your finger, just keep your finger in place when you start working on the sound exercises.
- It's important to have enough space for the air and sound to come out of your mouth, so don't place your little finger in the center of your mouth.

Trying Out Body Sounds

- Check that your face and even your eyes are drooping in a very relaxed way. You should have that yawn feeling, your chin should be released. Redo these checks often.
- The first sound I want you to make is a simple pant or what I call a Body Sound. Don't think of *using* your throat to *make* it happen. It's the kind of sound you might make with your whole body after you've been running a short distance—a soft, panting **UH** that feels primitive or animal-like (see figure 10).
- Your tongue should be flat and slightly concave, with the tip against your lower teeth.
- Your inhalation can be lightly audible or silent as you draw your breath in through an open throat.
- Exhale with a deep, almost groaning sound.
- The rhythm should be steady, about one second for the inhalation and the same for the exhalation.
- The gentle Body Breathing Muscle action of your Body Breath powers your breath and sound.
- Three or four pants, a swallow to moisturize your throat, then a short rest, sets up a good practicing balance.

Tips for Practicing Panting UH Body Sounds

If your throat gets dry, you should swallow more throughout and intermittently drink some water. If your throat hurts or feels hoarse when you pant these sounds, you should relax it with a yawn. Any sense of roughness is usually caused by tension in your throat or by an unconscious or habitual reliance on your throat, instead of your Body Breathing Muscle, to support the sound.

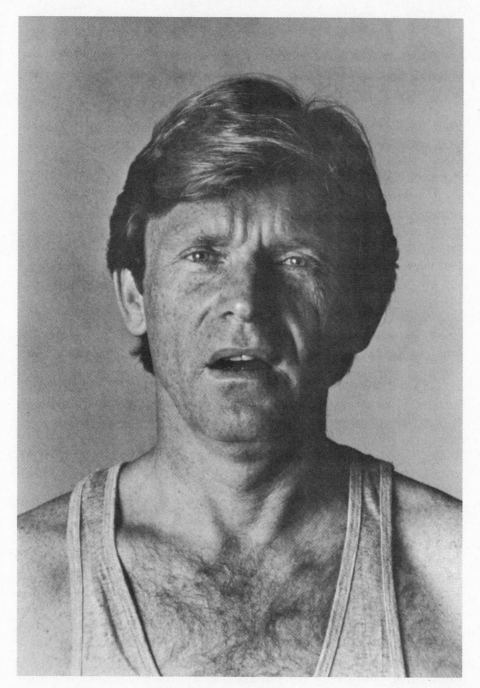

Figure 10. Panting the UH Body Sound

You may get lightheaded if you pant too many times with no rest in between. This can happen because you're inhaling more oxygen than you're used to in a short amount of time. If you find yourself getting dizzy, just stop panting until the feeling goes away, and continue less exuberantly.

Notice that the sound doesn't involve any action in your throat. Your neck should feel wide and soft, both inside and out. Imagine that your sound is originating deep inside the lowest part of your torso, with your Body Breathing Muscle pumping that sound through your body.

Imagine your throat and neck as being there only to *receive* the sound your Body Breathing Muscle pumps through your body. They stay passive while your Body Breathing Muscle gently activates your inhaling and exhaling. Through it all your face should look and feel very soft, like warm dough.

If you pant in groups of three or four with the one-second inhalation, one-second exhalation tempo, you won't have time between the inhalation and the exhalation to let your mind or throat revert to their old way of organizing sound. The panting **UH** should be much deeper than what you normally think of as your speaking sound.

Your Body Sound should feel like it originates in your lower torso, sending the major vibration to your upper chest. Your throat is also vibrating in a much milder way. And if you're making the sounds correctly, your voice won't crack. Sound is vibration. And when your voice cracks, there's a break in that vibration, like a glitch. You won't get those glitches if you are relaxed and your throat is not getting into the act.

It might help you to understand the difference between a throat sound and a Body Sound better if you deliberately *make* a throat sound. Tighten your vocal cords and neck muscles and say "Er, Er," in a middle-range tone. You should sound like a crow. Do you feel and hear how different this is from your panting sound? (See figure 11.)

If your sound is still in your throat, try lightly hitting your sternum (just below your collar bones) with your fist while making your **UH** Body Sound. It should resemble an Indian chant.

You may want to stay with the **UH** panting sounds for a few days until your body sensations correspond to the ones I've described, and then try the **OH**, **AH**, and **AY** Body Sounds.

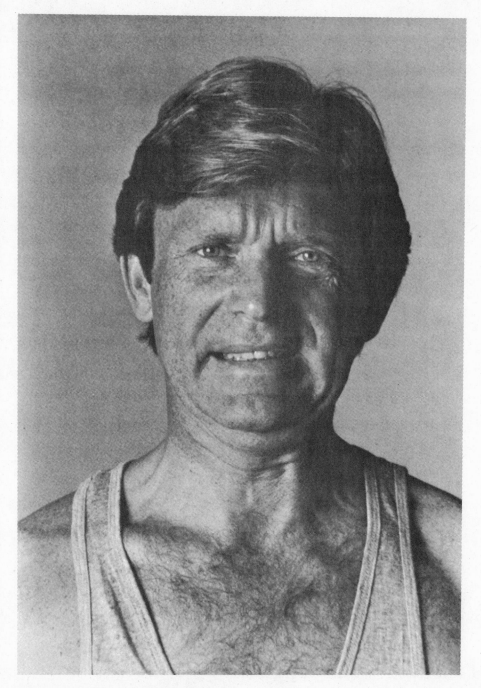

*Figure 11. Making the **ER** Throat Sound*

Producing UH + OH, AH and AY Body Sounds

Expanding your panting experience with more sounds will move you that much closer to Body Speaking.

Preparation

- Body Breathe using your Body Breathing Muscle. Your chin is still soft, with your little finger between your teeth if you need it to keep your mouth and teeth apart. Your throat has a yawn feeling. Your tongue is slightly concave as you make the sounds.
- Begin by panting a few UH's, just to get yourself started. Remember, you want to keep that dough-faced expression on your face, your mouth slightly open, and your throat and neck relaxed.
- You should not change the position of your mouth or the expression of your face as you change from the UH to an OH; just think OH with your mind. It should *feel* just like the UH.

Trying an OH

- Try panting three or four OH's, just exactly the way you panted the UH. Watch yourself in a mirror to see whether your face stays the same when you switch from UH to OH. Try not to shape the OH with your mouth.
- It may help you to imagine that you are sending these sounds from your lower body to your upper chest, causing it to vibrate. You should be able to feel the vibration from all of these sounds if you put your hand on your chest. It might help you to actually imagine your mouth located in your upper chest, about three inches below the indentation between your collar bones.
- Do as many panting groups as you need to experience the OH the way you felt the UH Body Sound. Deep, rich, solid. Don't attempt to add to your volume yet. Try practicing it now five or ten times.

Shift to an AH

- Experiment with the AH sound.
- Don't change your face, lips, or tongue.
- Just think AH, inhale audibly or silently, and then exhale an AH.
- Repeat until you have a sense of this Body Sound.

AY Is Slightly Different

- Your tongue should be flat and slightly concave when you make the **UH, OH,** and **AH** sounds, but when you move on to the **AY,** your tongue bumps up just a bit in the middle, and the tip rests gently against your lower teeth (see figure 12).
- Remember how gangsters sound in some movies? "A-a-y, you guys, a-a-y." That's the kind of sound I want you to make—slightly crude and rough.

From Panting Groups to Single Sounds

The final step in practicing Body Sounds is to move from panting to more resonant sounds.

Single Body Sounds

- Now inhale a *silent*, open-throated Body Breath and exhale a single **UH** about one second long, rather than panting a group of three or four.
- The sound should be richer and fuller than it is when you are panting the Body Sounds, with slightly more power from your Body Breathing Muscle (see figure 13).
- Try several single **UH**'s, with an inhale for each **UH**.
- Move on to a series of single **OH**'s, then **AH**'s, then **AY**'s.

Tips for Practicing Body Sounds

When you begin to change from panting sounds to producing single sounds, you may have a tendency to overdo the Body Breathing Muscle movement. Even though your single Body Sounds should be fuller, with more power from your breathing, don't think you need an overly large breathing movement. In fact, the movement of your Body Breathing Muscle should still be relatively small.

Think of the balance between your breathing movement and your Body Sounds like a seesaw. Maintaining a rhythm of breathing in and exhaling sounds is like having two people of similar weight, one on each end of the plank, alternating up and down. Making a large Body Breathing Muscle movement is like putting a huge adult on one end of the seesaw and a small child on the other. It's likely to

Figure 12. Mouth Positions for Body Sound Exercises

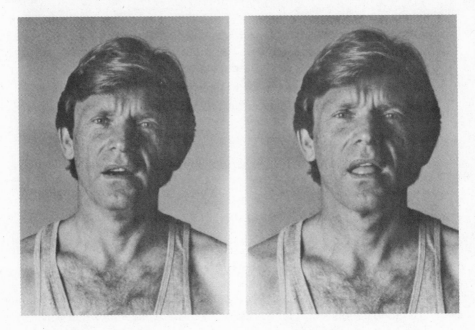

*A. Mouth Position for **UH, OH,** and **AH**   B. Mouth Position for **AY***

interfere with the rhythm of your breathing and prevent you from releasing a relaxed, full sound.

I suggest you practice these Body Sounds until you feel secure with them before going on to the next stage. It may take only a few days or possibly a few weeks to get some of the basic techniques down. Becoming more aware of your body, emotional nature, and stress levels can take several months. But mastering Body Breathing and Body Sounds should not take long. Keep working on these exercises, and you'll start feeling more and more at home with them.

And be patient with yourself. You need *time* to absorb your new body/breathing/sound experiences.

Body Sound Exercises—Quick Reference Chart

● Breathe in gently with your Body Breathing Muscle, making a lightly audible **UH** sound on the inhalation if you can (if not, inhale silently). Exhale with a deep, primal **UH** Body Sound. Pant three or four times, swallow, then rest. Your mouth should be partly open, your face loose and soft, your tongue slightly concave, and your throat wide.

Figure 13. Body Breathing Movement

A. *Body Breathing Movement for Soft Sounds*

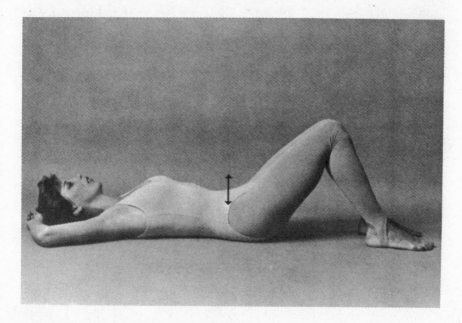

B. *Body Breathing Movement for Louder Sounds*

- Imagine your Body Sound starting at the bottom of your torso and exiting from your upper chest as if your mouth were there. Check the vibration with your hand when you make the Body Sound.
- Without changing your face or body, change your sound by thinking **OH**. Practice **OH**'s in a series as you did the **UH**'s. Then do a series of **AH**'s. When you move to **AY**, be sure to bump up the middle of your tongue. Then do the **OH**'s, **AH**'s, and **AY**'s in rotation, following the panting sequence described above.
- Inhale a silent Body Breath, and exhale a single, richer sound on the **UH, OH, AH,** and **AY**, taking about one second for the inhalation and one second for the exhaled Body Sound.

Here are some special exercises which will show you more ways to relax your throat and upper chest. They will also expand the way you experience your BodyVoice. Try each one a few times.

- Tighten your vocal cords as much as you can without making a sound and then let them go, several times in sequence. Yawn.
- Hit your sternum below your collar bone lightly with your fist, while making your **UH** Body Sound. It should resemble Indian chanting.
- Put your thumb on one side of the front of your throat and your fingers on the other side, very gently, and see if there is a forward and slightly downward movement when you make the **UH** sound. If not, try to get that to happen.
- Ask someone to press firmly on your sternum while you exhale air out of your upper chest. Three times should be enough.

eleven
Lower Body Support

These next techniques will teach you how to support your voice with your legs and lower torso—showing you how to use the biggest muscles in your body for your Body Sound. This support is twofold:

For the physical activity of breathing and speaking
For the full energetic expression of yourself

Most people are aware of the supportive strength and energy in their feet, calves, thighs, and buttocks when doing physical work, exercises, or sports. However, they seldom realize that the same muscles can and should support how they breathe and speak.

And many who are conscious of the sensations in their sexual anatomy during sexual arousal do not realize that sexual-energetic aliveness is an integral part of feeling physically alive throughout the day. In fact, when you speak, the presence of this quality in your voice helps to communicate charisma and vitality.

If you can become aware of this muscular and energetic grounding in your lower body during everyday activities, you will feel more supported and alive in all facets of your life. Even when you're using your mind, there's no need to cut yourself off from the sensory awareness and connection with the lower half of your anatomy.

The Lower Body Support Exercise—Lying Down

- Lie on your back, with your knees bent.
- Continue to use your Body Breathing Muscle to breathe.

175

- Keep your throat open and your face, neck, and shoulders relaxed, as before.
- Inhale a Body Breath, but this time when you exhale your **UH** Body Sound, push your feet firmly on the floor or bed.
- Don't lift your hips, but do let the movement of your legs tilt your pelvis gently, so that the small of your back comes down flat as you release your **UH**.
- Try this five times.
- You should feel energy moving from the bottom of your feet up through your torso as you release your sound. Notice how this action puts your Body Sound in closer contact with the lower part of your body.
- Do you sense the powerful connection between your legs, thighs, pelvis, genitals, and buttocks and your voice as you release your Body Sound through your torso, neck and mouth? Try this exercise again focusing on sensing all these areas.

The Lower Body Support Exercise—Sitting Up

You can do the same exercise sitting in a chair:

- Take a Body Breath, push your feet on the floor as before, and let your thighs and pelvis respond just as they did when you were lying down.
- This lower body movement is like the small forward "bump" of a dancer.
- Most people eventually feel warm sexual-energetic sensations when they practice their Body Sounds if their full body energy is releasing.

Further Variations

Variations that can be done lying down or sitting in a chair:

- Take an inventory of your body. Then focus on the general sensations in your genitals. It might be sensuous, warm, cool, contracted, or just nothing at all.
- Tilt your pelvis and exhale an **UH**, as you contract your genitals.
- Try that a few more times.
- Try several **UH** sounds as you contract your buttocks.
- Then, conversely, experiment with pushing your anus or genitals gently downward as your release the **UH.**

- Now sense your genitals again and note any changes in energetic quality.
- Do these techniques with **OH, AH,** and **AY**.

Special Tips for Drawing on Your Lower Body Support

Your upper torso above your navel should remain passive, simply vibrating with the sound produced by this lower body action. Be sure your vocal cords or neck muscles don't contract when you push your feet to move your lower body. If they do, use the exercises described in Chapter 10 to release and relax them.

The idea is to work the energy and muscles of your feet, thighs, buttocks, crotch (anus and genitals), and pelvis so that your voice is supported by your lower body, allowing your throat to receive sound in a relaxed way (see figure 14).

Consider the muscles in the lower part of your body as the "big guns"—far more capable of supporting your voice than the relatively small muscles of your throat and neck.

Visualize a wide tube or a periscope coming from your crotch up through your body and neck, across a concave tongue and out of your mouth. That's the route the **UH, OH, AH,** and **AY** Body Sounds travel.

Lower Body Support Exercises—Quick Reference Chart

- Inhale a Body Breath and as you exhale, push firmly on the floor with your feet, allowing your pelvis to tilt gently upward as you exhale the **UH** sound.
- Check to see if your upper body and throat are tensing or contracting as you make these sounds, and use the relaxation techniques, if necessary.
- Practice the **UH, OH, AH,** and **AY** sounds singly, using this lower body movement.
- Notice the energy and sensations in your legs, crotch, and pelvis. Experience the sound of your voice as a part of your sexual-energetic body aliveness.

Figure 14. Lower Body Support for Body Sounds

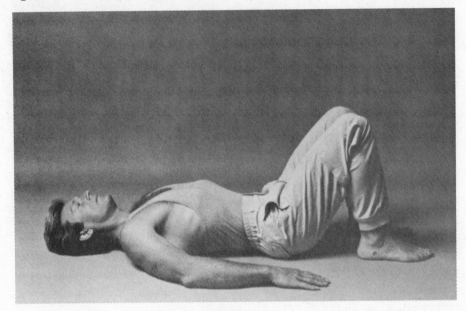

A. *Position Before Inhaling a Body Breath*

B. *As you exhale a Body Sound, push your feet against the floor. The small of your back moves down.*

twelve

Baby Motor Drill

The Baby Motor Drill is a technique for practicing the exhalation of sound and air at the same time. It will show you how to keep a workable balance between the two, so you can take full advantage of the natural vibration of your vocal cords as you speak. This drill will also teach you to connect the movement of your Body Breathing Muscle with nonverbal sound (in preparation for talking), and expand your breathing capacity.

Most people close their throats as they speak, limiting their sound and breath. When you become proficient with the Baby Motor Drill, and can exhale long Body Breaths with sound through an open throat—while both lips, or your tongue and lower lip, are vibrating—you will be combining sound and breath efficiently.

You're going to be sipping air in through your mouth, expanding first the area below your navel, then your midsection, your lower chest, and your upper chest. Your torso should feel as if you were filling a balloon or stuffing a sausage with air. You'll be making a sipping sound with your lips as you bring the air into your body.

Your Body Breathing Muscle should stay out once it's filled with air. Your midsection should also stay out once it's filled. So be sure *not* to pull in your Body Breathing Muscle as you inhale into your lower and upper chest, as some people have a tendency to do.

You will learn this drill in three steps:

The sipping breath
The **MMM** sound
The "baby motor" sound

179

Step 1: The Sipping Breath

Sip your breath into your body in four stages as shown in figure 15:

- With the first sip, you expand the gut area below your navel just as you did with the Body Breath.
- With the second sip, the area directly above your navel fills with breath.
- The third sip fills the lower chest and the fourth expands your upper chest.
- Exhale normally and repeat the sipping inhale a few times.

Step 2: The MMM Sound

In this step you will add a long, soft, exhaled hum with an **MMM** sound to the extended inhalation you have been practicing.

- With your teeth slightly apart and your lips closed, ready to make a humming sound, try an easy, soft **MMM** tone for a few seconds. You should feel a lot of space in your mouth and a yawn in your throat as you practice this.
- Now take a "four-sip" breath, using the Body Breathing Muscle action described above, and hum for as long as you can as you *slowly* exhale.
- When you try the extended exhalation with humming, the goal is for your Body Breathing Muscle to stay out for as long as possible. If it starts to come back in early in the exercise, just push it back out.
- When you feel you need the air in the bottom of your lungs, gently and slowly float your Body Breathing Muscle in toward your spine. Your Body Breathing Muscle should not be rigid, but should feel like a rubber ball floating on water.
- While the air and sound are flowing very slowly out of your body, your upper chest should feel a little as if you were holding your breath under water. You should have a mild sense of compression—as if you were blowing up a balloon that is resisting your breath.
- Try this a few times and then time yourself. Your target time for good breath control is about twenty to twenty-five seconds—which can take a few weeks of practice to achieve. When you come to the end of your breath, be careful not to contract your face, neck, or shoulders.

You are stuffing yourself with air to increase your lung capacity and holding your breath back as much as possible in order to learn how

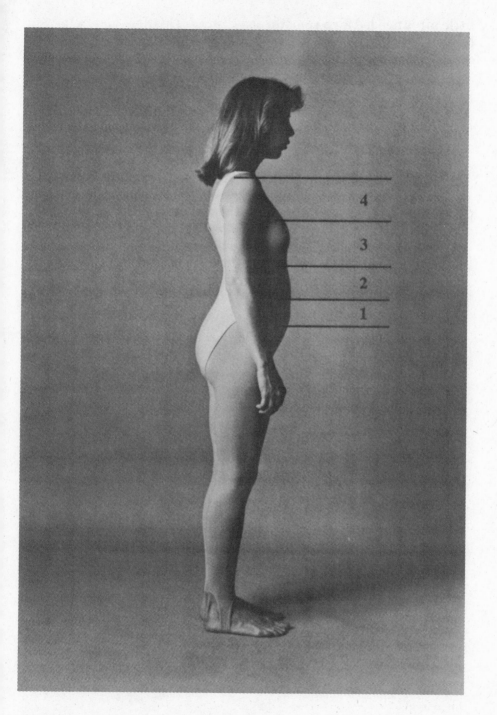

Figure 15. The Four Stage Sipping Breath

little air is needed for a smooth, easy sound. This drill also helps you to experience how the action of the Body Breathing Muscle is connected to your breath and sound in Body Speaking.

Step 3: The "Baby Motor" Sound

- First experiment by pursing your lips together, kiss-kiss fashion.
- Take an easy Body Breath. Watch yourself in a mirror.
- Your aim is to combine your humming sound with the **B-B-B-B-B-B** sound of your vibrating lips on one continuous exhalation of sound and breath. You should sound like a little motor boat or a baby experimenting with sounds (see figure 16A).
- Putting your fingers gently on your cheeks or to the sides of your mouth is a big help in directing the air toward your lips (see figure 16B).

Figure 16. The Baby Motor Drill

 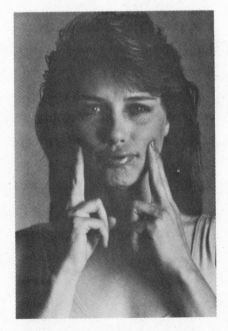

A. *Vibrating Lips and Making the*   B. *Using Fingers on Cheeks to Help*
B-B-B-B *Sound*

Practice vibrating your lips with sound. Then experiment with the following variation:

- Put your tongue out of your mouth over your lower lip, and place your upper teeth down lightly on the center of your tongue (see figure 17).
- Exhale sound and air out under your tongue, seeing if you can make your tongue and lower lip vibrate.
- You may find one technique easier than the other, but continue to experiment with both.

Don't give up if your lips and tongue don't work as you want them to immediately. Practice both techniques in a relaxed way over a period of time. Some people find that it helps them to try this drill in the shower with the water running over their mouths. But if you don't have success either with vibrating your lips, or your tongue and lower lip, after giving both a good try, simply practice the sipping breath with a hum instead.

When you have these basics down, try doing the exercise as you gaze at a distant horizon, and visualize an infinite supply of butterflies or bubbles coming out of your mouth. Or come up with some other mental image for yourself that makes the exercise more fun. Changing your focus in this way can help you relax into the drill and spend more time on it. It should feel soothing to your throat if you're doing it correctly.

The amount of air pressure you need to vibrate your lips, or your tongue and lower lip, prepares you for the breathing dynamics of Body Speaking. Eventually, you should feel you are talking by exhaling words on a slow, steady stream of air through an open throat, in somewhat the same way you handle your breath in this exercise. Don't worry about looking and sounding funny while you are doing this—it's worth it to acquire this valuable breath control technique.

With this exercise you rehearse sound, *without* words, in much the same way your Body Breath, open throat, relaxed jaw, and Body Sound will eventually work together *with* words—when you start Body Speaking.

Baby Motor Drill—Quick Reference Chart

- Sip the breath into your body in four stages, expanding your lower torso, midbody, lower chest, and then upper chest. Exhale.

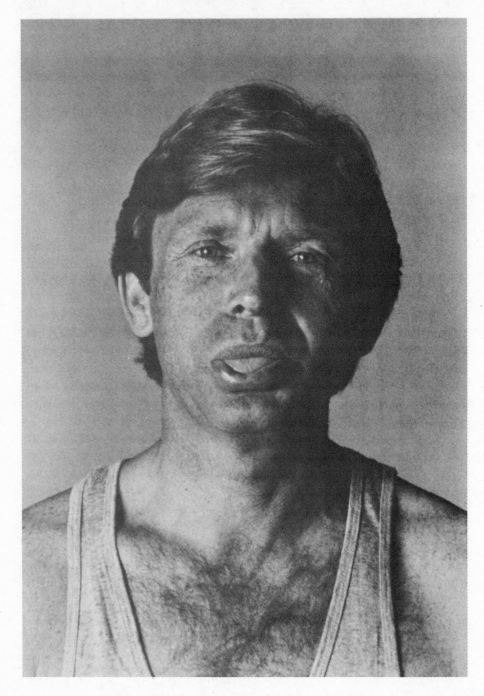

Figure 17. The Baby Motor Drill—Tongue Out Position

- Inhale the sipping breath, and hum softly as you exhale slowly. Keep your Body Breathing Muscle out as long as possible. Then float it slowly in toward your spine as you reach the end of your breath. See how long you can do this.
- Vibrate your lips with a humming sound while slowly exhaling your four stage breath.
- Try putting your tongue out of your mouth over your lower lip, placing your upper teeth down lightly on the center of your tongue and letting your breath flow out under your tongue, so that both your tongue and lower lip vibrate as you exhale. Practice the drill with both mouth positions, or choose the way that's more successful for you.

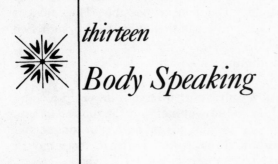

thirteen

Body Speaking

You're now ready to put together everything you've learned so far and to begin using your BodyVoice with words and sentences. To prepare for Body Speaking, you can review the steps you've taken up to this point: relaxing, BodyBreathing, producing Body Sounds with the support of your lower torso, and combining breath control and sound with the Baby Motor Drills.

In the following exercise you will practice with five basic Body Speaking sentences. This time you will exhale not just sounds, but words, as you release air and sound from your body. You'll learn to Body Speak in three steps:

Speaking sentences without inflection, beginning with a **HO** or **OH** Body Sound

Adding inflection

Dropping the initial **HO** or **OH**

Step 1: The Body Speaking Sentences

The five simple sentences you will use to practice Body Speaking are:

HO,-Hi-how-are-you?
HO,-Gee-it's-a-great-day.
HO,-Hey-thanks-a-lot.

186

HO,-G'bye-take-care.
HO,-Hello-this-is-(your first name).

- Start each sentence with a **HO**, as indicated, or an **OH**—whichever works better for you.
- It should sound just like the single **UH, OH, AH,** and **AY** Body Sounds. The idea is to carry the **OH** or **HO** caveman sound over into the rest of the sentence, so that every word you speak seems to come directly from the bottom of your torso, up through your body, and out of your mouth.
- As you practice, put one hand on your Body Breathing Muscle so you can be sure you're inhaling fully and so you can feel it moving slowly *in*, as the words of the sentence move up and out of your body.
- Visualize that the words are all connected to each other, as if they were in one liquid stream.
- Try to be sure there's no break in sound between the **OH** or **HO** and the first word of the sentence.
- There should be no breaks between the words in the sentence either.
- The tempo should be slow; draw out the vowels and take about *three and a half seconds* for each sentence. The last one will vary with the length of your first name.

Use your tongue and the action of your lower jaw to articulate the words, with no distortion in the pronunciation of any of the words.

- Keep your face expressionless and very relaxed.
- Think of your lower jaw as being made of marshmallows, dropping down vertically like a puppet's jaw to let your words come out. You almost shut your mouth by closing your lower jaw between words as your tongue takes on the responsibility of enunciating.
- Your upper lip is soft, but does *not* take various shapes for the different words—it stays the same for all of them.
- During the first step you will be delivering the sentences in a *monotone*. Once again, try to sound very much like a caveman— whether you're a man or a woman (see figures 18 and 19).

When you practice the sentences, it helps to hold the side of your face and jaw with one of your hands to keep your lower mouth and jaw slack, but mobile. Put your other hand on your Body Breathing Muscle to check your Body Breathing.

If you find you are distorting the pronunciation of the words,

Figure 18. Jaw Movements for Step 1 & Step 2 of Body Speaking Practice

 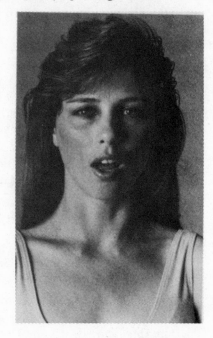

A. Mouth Position to Begin and Between Words   *B. Mouth Position When Saying Words*

say the sentences as you normally would, noticing the action of your tongue. Then keep your tongue moving in the same way for the exercise, but slower.

Step 2: Adding Inflection

Step 2 is just like Step 1 except that this time *you add inflection*, rather than speaking in a monotone. You are moving toward more normal speech by giving the sentences some intonation, but you keep your drawn-out, caveman sound and dough-faced expression.

- Use the **OH** or **HO** to begin each sentence, as before.
- The sentences are short, so none of them should require all your breath.
- Be sure your upper chest resonates with sound, and imagine that your words are emerging from your upper torso, if that idea helps.
- Follow the same timing you used for Step 1.

Figure 19. Facial Expression While Practicing Body Breathing—Steps 1 and 2

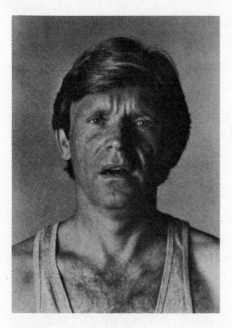

A. *"HO"*

B. *"HI, HOW"*

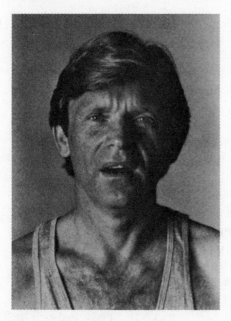

C. *"ARE"*

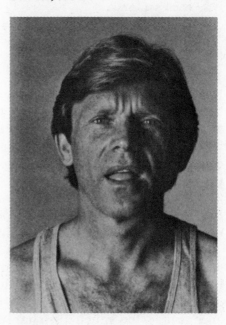

D. *"YOU?"*

HO,-Hi-how-are-you?
HO,-Gee-it's-a-great-day.
HO,-Hey-thanks-a-lot.
HO,-G'bye-take-care.
HO,-Hello-this-is-(your first name).

Step 3: Dropping the HO or OH

Now, you'll be saying the sentences *without* the **OH** or **HO** in front, using a tempo, melody, and phrasing normal for you. No more caveman sound—civilization is coming! This time you'll want your face to look normal too. Practice smiling with your mouth and your eyes as you say the sentences—you can't sound friendly unless you look that way! Just be sure your BodyVoice still feels like it's coming from your lower torso. Release a small amount of Body Breath as you speak the words and continue to string them together, but in a way that sounds normal and natural.

- The first syllable of each sentence should *feel* like the **HO** or **OH** in Steps 1 and 2, but *sound* more refined. It should be the lowest note in each sentence.
- Use the **Hi**, the **He** of hello, the **Gee**, the **Hey**, and the **G's** of g'bye to springboard the rest of the words up from your Body Breathing Muscle.

Beginning each sentence with good, low BodyVoice support will give the rest of the sentence a chance to stay connected to the lower part of your body. This doesn't mean that eventually all your speaking will have to begin with a deep tone; it's just a useful technique to stay connected to your BodyVoice when you practice these Body Speaking techniques.

Be sure you don't push your voice down in your throat to get it low. Your sound should start from low in your body and resonate mostly in your lower neck and throat.

For Step 3, each of the first four sentences should take about *one and a half seconds*, with a variation on the last if your first name is more than one syllable. Your lips should not move in an exaggerated way to pronounce the words, the way many speech classes encourage—too much lip shaping *inhibits* your vocal tone. The clarity of Body Speaking comes from good tongue and teeth articulation. Putting your forefinger across your upper lip when you rehearse the sentences will help to soften overactive mouth movements.

Your tone should start low, then rise in the middle of the sentence, then become low again as you finish the words. Sometimes it helps to inhale a silent **OH** before you exhale the sentence, in order to widen your throat as you breathe in. You can feel your vocal cords open as you inhale the breath, as you would if you were yawning. Keep that same open-throat yawn feeling when you exhale the sentence.

Breathing Overview for Body Speaking

As you pant the **UH**'s, **OH**'s, **AH**'s, and **AY**'s on a Body Breath, you should exhale enough air to feel a slight breeze if you put your hand in front of your mouth.

When making the separate, single Body Sounds through a relaxed throat, your hand should detect less air coming out of your mouth.

In practicing the Baby Motor Drill correctly, you release even less air, as you focus your efforts on maintaining a continuous tone, while controlling your Body Breath with your Body Breathing Muscle.

When you start speaking actual words, you will modify the Body Sound and Baby Motor Drill techniques, using a bit less air than you needed with the **UH**'s, **OH**'s, **AH**'s, and **AY**'s, but about the same amount you required for the Baby Motor Drill. Your sound and air combination should feel balanced when you do the Body Speaking sentences. You should not feel that you are compressing the air in your chest or consciously holding your air back. When you put your hand in front of your mouth while saying the sentences, you should feel very little breath coming out.

Tips for Body Speaking

The first four sentences are good ways to rehearse your Body-Voice under circumstances when no one will expect your voice to sound one way or another—the grocery store, the drug store, the cleaners, or the gas station. So they are useful when you want to try your new voice out in the world without feeling self-conscious. The last sentence is particularly suited for the telephone, but most people find that practicing all the sentences is easier during telephone conversations, at first.

After a while, you'll want to make up short sentences of your own that will fit your particular daily routine; ones you know you'll use often at home and at work. Be sure to practice them first according to the methods outlined in Steps 1, 2, and 3.

Some people are shy about trying their new BodyVoice. Your personal reaction may be:

It doesn't sound like me.
It sounds too low.
I am so self-conscious, I must sound affected.
It feels too breathy. (Other people won't hear it that way, however.)

Or people you know may offer their own comments at first. It's no small thing to change your voice and yourself, and it may take a while for you and those around you to come to terms with what you are achieving. However, the rewards of staying with your BodyVoice are too far-reaching to allow such considerations to hold you back.

With constant practice these techniques will become second nature to you and soon you'll find you're using your new BodyVoice spontaneously, enjoying a freely released Body Sound and Body Breathing in your healthy and successful way of Body Speaking.

Body Speaking Exercises—Quick Reference Chart

- Put one hand on your jaw to remove any tenseness, while your other hand on your lower torso feels the Body Breathing Muscle controlling your breath.
- Put an **OH** or **HO** in front of each practice sentence (see below).
- When you are comfortable with the sentences spoken in a monotone, drop the **OH** or **HO** in front and speak them with natural inflections.
- Inhale a silent **OH** at the beginning of each sentence, to widen your throat and use the first syllable of each sentence as if it were your **HO**—to springboard your BodyVoice into the rest of the sentence.

These are the sentences:

Hi-how-are-you?
Gee-it's-a-great-day.
Hey-thanks-a-lot.
G'bye-take-care.
Hello-this-is-(your first name).

fourteen
Body Voice Warm-Ups

Up to this point, all the exercises have been to *release your voice* so that you speak with a natural, inhaling-exhaling, organic process. Once that is accomplished, the BodyVoice warm-ups can be used to further *enhance the sound* of your voice. Be sure to prepare yourself with the other exercises *before* doing any warm-ups. If your voice has a good resonant sound at this point in your development, very little warming up will be necessary. But if you're like most people, including myself, a good twenty-minute warm-up will dramatically enrich your vocal quality.

Just as a musician warms up before a concert, or a runner before a race, it's important to take some preparation time if you want to bring out your best vocal quality and keep your voice healthy. Even when an athlete is in top form, all of his reflexes conditioned to perfection, he knows that his muscles need to be warmed up each day. And if it's the day of the big competition, he knows that it's important to take time to relax emotionally as well, to release tension, put fears and worries aside, and get himself into a winning frame of mind. The same is true of your voice for you to be your best as a communicator.

The most important principle to keep in mind for these warm-up exercises is that you should spend enough time so that your throat feels open and comfortable, your body relaxed, and your vocal sound full and confident. This is not a mechanical process like filling the gas tank or turning on a light. You have to be aware of how you feel and how you sound, and continue the warm-ups as long as necessary. Some days your voice will be in better shape than others, and so the amount of time you need to warm up your voice will vary from day to day.

Two sets of warm-up exercises are given below:

Basic BodyVoice warm-ups
Additional warm-up exercises for gaining the support of your lower body for your BodyVoice

Basic BodyVoice Warm-Up Exercises

The first thing to remember in warming up your BodyVoice is to start from the emotional-physical condition you are in. Don't pretend to be in any state you are not. Instead, take some time to enjoy the release that can come by acknowledging what's actually occurring in you at the moment. If you are emotionally upset, don't ignore it. Start from whatever you're experiencing.

After going through the basic preparations you've already learned, begin by easing into Body Sounds. Taking it gently and responsively is very important. If you're angry, tired, sleepy, or feeling aggressive, consider softer sounds mandatory for beginning your vocal warm-up. Let your emotions shape how you release the sounds. Moan, groan, grouch, coo, sigh into the sounds—but do it softly, gently, and let your emotions express themselves.

Step 1: HO's or OH's

- Decide for yourself which Body Sound syllable—**HO** or **OH**—works best for you. It may be easier for you to release the sound without an initial H.
- Crescendo from soft to loud, imagining you're going deeper in tone as you get louder—even though you're staying on the same sound. Do a series of crescendos as long as it feels appropriate.

Step 2: HUH's

- Do a **HUH** Body Sound and allow the sound to build up to an even louder volume than before.
- Try the same thing using short, staccato sounds—like a football player calling the signals.

Step 3: Short-Long

- Do a **HUH** in a combination short and long sound: **HUH-HUHHHHHHHH**.

Step 4: Drop in Pitch

- Do a **HEE-E-E-EH** sound (like the sounds Ed McMahon frequently makes on the Carson show before or after his famous "He-e-e-ere's Johnny").
- Start with a comfortable basic Body Sound and then drop in pitch. Massage the tone back and forth.

Step 5: HO-HA-HEH

- Massage these tones back and forth.

Step 6: Sentences

- Pick a sentence that you'll use soon after the warm-up, like, "Hello, my name is . . ." Use it like a litmus test, every five minutes, to see what your warm-ups are doing to your speaking voice.
- If your voice gets fluffy-sounding or too breathy, go to the **ER** or **EE** sounds, gently contracting your throat at the place between your collar bones.

Step 7: Baby Motor Drills

- Do the Baby Motor Drills intermittently.

Swallow a lot in between the various steps, and take moments of silence to moisten and relax your throat. Ten minutes to half an hour may be sufficient, but take as long as you need. If you're new at this, your warmed up voice may last an hour. If you're used to the techniques, it can last all day.

Lower Body Support Warm-Ups

Relaxation, Body Breathing, and awareness of your body energies are the ways you can get the support of your lower body for your voice—the strength of the big muscles of your thighs, buttocks, and legs, and the flow of sexual aliveness and finer energies (see figure 20). But when you're warming up your voice, there are some things you can do to give yourself a pick-me-up and get that energy flowing. Just like an athlete has laps in the swimming pool or around the track to get loosened up and energized, you can do some quick exercises to help energize your body in a way that will support your BodyVoice. These exercises will help you quickly to summon that sense of groundedness that is so important.

Try the following:

- Stamp or kick your feet as you practice producing Body Sounds. Be aware of the connection between the power in your legs and the support for your voice. These are not isolated, disconnected parts of your body, but an integrated whole. You want to feel the strength in your legs at the same time you feel the power of your BodyVoice—these experiences are part of the full-body flow of natural energies.

- Make cheerleading or other athletic motions with your arms and upper body (see figure 21). If you're in a car, you can punch the seat with your fist. Also, push against the floor of the car with your legs and feet, and practice your Body Sounds. Again, let yourself experience the movements of your muscles, the flow of energy in your arms and legs, and the sound of your voice as part of your full-body experience.

- Slap your thighs as you practice a speech. Feel the blood tingling in your legs. If you are very tired and distracted, or emotionally upset, slap yourself hard enough to feel a mild twinge of pain. Pain can be a great help in drawing your attention away from thoughts and feelings that are bothering you and bringing your attention back to your experience of your body. Don't overdo it!

When and Where to Do Warm-Ups

BodyVoice warm-ups should be performed whenever you need them to keep your voice released. However, few of us have the luxuries of unlimited time and privacy.

Figure 20. Pyramid of Energies

Figure 21. Energized Body Movements for Practicing Loud Body Sounds

If you drive to work, the half hour to hour you spend in your car commuting to and from home and office is an ideal time. What do you usually do with this time in your car? Listen to the radio? Sing? Daydream? One of the great practicalities of the Kenley Method is its portability. Sitting behind the wheel of your car is a perfectly acceptable position for going through the De-Stresser Technique, Body Breathing, and doing your BodyVoice warm-ups. After all, I discovered the BodyVoice while driving in my car en route to a job. Your car offers you privacy, too, much more than an apartment. If you're in heavy traffic, just roll up your windows, and you can make any kind of sounds you want, at any volume. There's no one upstairs or downstairs or on the other side of a thin wall to inhibit you or complain to your landlord.

Do your warm-ups where it's most convenient for you, but be sure you do them. They are an essential step in developing your BodyVoice.

fifteen
Contacting Your Finer Energies

Contact with the finer energies in your body will bring even more natural aliveness and personal uniqueness into the sound of your speaking voice. The exercises in this step of the Kenley Method are really guides to help you become aware of your more inner body energies and their emotional interrelationships. You can incorporate this enhanced awareness into your communication on many levels and, as you master this part of the techniques, your voice—and your life—will be enriched.

Awareness—focused attention with curiosity and acceptance—is the key to experiencing these finer body energies. Consider the energy of your muscles as a rough external fabric in comparison with the more silklike texture of these refined internal energies. As indicated in figure 22, I am referring to the essential personal qualities of:

Strength and support
Self-sufficiency
Will power and determination
Love and compassion
Self-expression and creativity
Mental clarity
Joy

Exploring these parts of yourself requires patience. You may welcome new inner experiences, but at some point you might feel

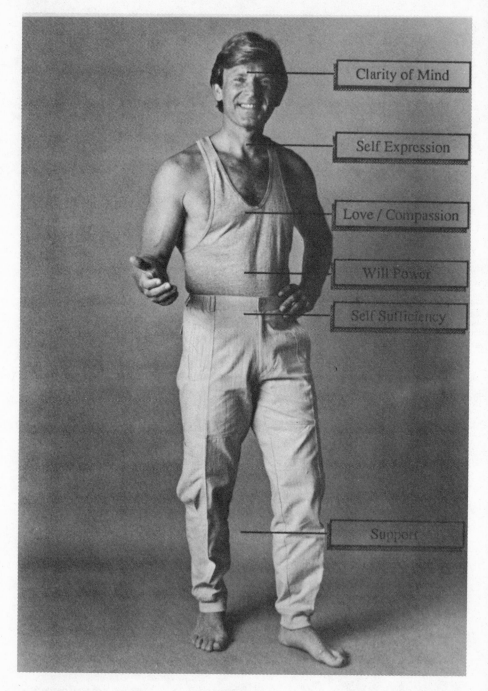

Figure 22. Finer Energies in Body Speaking

resistance to opening up or to letting go of old patterns of thinking and behavior. If so, you might want to investigate deeper facets of your self-discovery by seeking a private teacher. There's really no substitute for personal instruction or the support and structure that workshops and seminars can provide.

You can begin to develop these energies by working on them one at a time. You can proceed in three stages:

Locating and investigating the energetic quality in your body
Developing a daily focus on this energy
Producing Body Sounds that reflect the quality of this energy

Basics for Locating Your Finer Energies

The basic technique for locating and investigating each of your finer body energies is to focus your thoughts on a particular energetic quality. You'll do this in a way very similar to the BodyVoice relaxation exercise that you learned earlier as part of the De-Stresser Technique. There you explored the internal physical sensations of your arms and legs. Here you'll be sensing your physical and emotional states with the intention of moving toward the inner capacities that reflect more of your essential nature.

You'll be identifying what is happening at the moment related to the quality you're investigating, and recalling any kinds of experiences that closed down this energy and ones that made it feel more present. By employing the suggestions in the table on pages 204–206, you will probably begin to have some experience of this finer body energy.

If you feel "nothing," accept that internal sense as your initial experience on the way toward discovery. There is no right or wrong way to progress in this self-exploration. What you experience is what is valid for you. Sensory awareness of any finer body energy comes gradually and subtly. That's why they are often referred to as *subtle* qualities.

The following steps will show you how to locate each of your finer body energies:

• Decide which energy you want to focus on.

- Refer to the table on pages 204–206. There you will find specific instructions for how to get in touch with and recognize the emergence of this internal energy.
- Allow yourself to develop a felt sensory perception of the quality of this energy.

Table for Locating Your Finer Energies

Energetic Quality	Body Focus	How to Locate and Recognize
Support, Strength	Lower spine, Legs	Lie on a firm bed or mattress. With your legs straight and heels flexed, kick very hard, scissor-fashion, for as long as you can. Lie still and sense the energy that flows through your body. It can feel strong, red in color, energized, hot. You can consider this a way of tapping into the source of strength and power your lower spine and legs can activate for you. This can also be done by stomping your feet on the floor when you're sitting or walking around.
Self-sufficiency, Personal presence	Lower abdomen	Lie down or sit and put your attention on your lower torso below your navel. Your Life Energy Center is a place inside your body located approximately two to four inches below your navel and at a depth of about two to four inches inside your pelvic cavity. Put your hands on this area. Focus your attention there and see what you can feel. You might sense a mild presence of energy, a warm sunny sensation, or a very subtle wave of movement. It can seem very small or wide and radiating. These perceptions can enhance your sense of fullness and completeness and give you a sense of intuitive knowing. It is the personally felt quality of your own human presence—the sense of "I am."
Will Power, Determination	Solar Plexus	Lie down with your knees bent. Do three short doggie pants and one long exhalation into the area between the bottom of

your ribs and navel. Do this sequence as long as you feel comfortable. If you find yourself getting lightheaded, or that you're tingling anywhere in your body, stop until these sensations subside. Notice what energy you feel in your solar plexus as a result of the breathing. Contemplate having a feeling of will power and determination at work in your life, and notice what inner qualities in this area respond. When will is present, it can feel cool, silverlike, moonlike, and solid. It has a flavor of purposefulness, the certainty that you can carry through.

Love, Compassion	Heart	Lie down on your bed and focus on your heart—is it full, expanded, and warm, or without much sensation? To activate energy and feeling in your chest, hit your elbows on the mattress for about thirty seconds and then check your heart sensations again. Breathe gently into your heart several times. Then think of something or someone you love now or have loved in the past and notice what happens to your heart energies. Try listening to a favorite piece of music that you find especially moving. The heart can respond by feeling fluffy, pink, and sweet. It can also feel like liquid, merging gold, or like a soft, green elixir if the sensation feels more like compassion than love.
Self-expression, Creativity	Throat	Your throat and the area between your collar bones can feel fully at ease when you have the openness to express yourself in every way, regardless of the situation. Make several soft **UH** sounds, then slowly increase the volume. Continue for several minutes with the idea of your own self-expression coming forward in both sound and feeling. Consider for the moment that anything you would have to say is valuable as you focus on this part of your body. Then say, first in a soft voice, "I sound wonderful." Continue to repeat

		this sentence, louder and louder. The color amber is associated with the release of the quality related to this expression.
Mental Clarity	Mind	Clarity is only possible when the mind reaches a state of quiet calmness. Lie down and breathe quickly and deeply until you feel slightly lightheaded. Then relax for a few moments. Next, look at the ceiling and imagine a large circle there. Continue to roll your eyes around that circle, right, down, left, up, about fifteen times in one direction; then reverse and repeat fifteen more times. Next, hum softly with an **M-M-M** or **N-N-N,** sending the sound to your forehead, right between your eyebrows, on your exhalation. Quietly perceive what you feel. The quality that comes with clarity of the mind is a sense of peace, which can be experienced as a deep black or a light, clear space.
Joy	Throughout your body	Joy can come by itself in special moments when something deeply touches your emotions—a beautiful painting, a passionate symphony, the birth of a baby, or falling in love. Joy can also accompany the realization of any of the other finer energies. As you reclaim your inner feelings of strength, self-sufficiency, will, love, creativity, and clarity, you may also experience the effervescent quality of joy. Joy can be felt as yellow, light, and sparkling.

Developing a Daily Focus

The development of these energies happens mostly by focused attention. They will emerge by simply asking yourself many times each day:

What do I feel regarding the quality of the energy I'm focusing on?

How can I precisely describe it in terms of sensations or images? When I am aware of this energy, how does it affect the way I behave? What does my voice feel and sound like when I'm in touch with this quality in myself?

The steps to contact your inner energies don't need to be complicated. But in order to cultivate these or other subtle sensations for yourself, your mental and physical attitude is very important. The following suggestions may be of help:

- Remember that all of your body energies are *you*. And that means you want to reach a point where you experience them fully—because it feels good, and it adds to your personal experience of yourself, others, and life. Contacting these qualities is not like doing a quick check on whether you have a headache, or your stomach's growling with hunger, or your muscles need a workout in a gym. You might think of it like having your eyes adjust to seeing in a darkened room just after you've turned out the lights. At first, there's only darkness, then vague shapes, and then finally a subtle world of suggested colors, shadows, and soft, glimmering objects.

- Be open and accepting when calling forth more experience of yourself. Setting up an agenda of certain expectations will only limit the possibilities. Just keep asking yourself what's going on throughout the day, during all your activities: when you get up, when you're having breakfast, when you're driving to work, when you're talking to your friends and associates, when you're alone, when you're in a conference—all the time.

- Be prepared to have the experience of your finer energies become an integral part of your expanded personal nature. You are going to know those feelings of aliveness in your body intimately. Enjoy them, rely on them—and wonder how you ever got along without them!

Producing Body Sounds that Reflect Your Finer Energies

Now it's time to focus your attention toward experiencing your finer body energies while you are producing Body Sounds.

- Lie down with your knees up, and go through your preparation for Body Sounds. Be sure you are relaxed and Body Breathing and that your mouth is in the slightly open position. Use your little finger to gauge the optimal space between your lips and teeth if this is helpful.

- Try a few soft **UH** or **AH** Body Sounds, whichever you prefer.
- As you continue your **UH** or **AH** sounds, focus your awareness and your sound on the inner energetic strength of your legs. Ask yourself the questions to identify what you are experiencing on a finely tuned level. Be open to inner sensory perceptions of strength and support while you let that energy, with the **UH** or **AH** sound, flow throughout your entire body.
- Ask yourself how your Body Sounds feel and sound with a sense of this quality. Particularly, observe your state of relaxation along with this energy. Imagine yourself speaking with this feeling in your body and say, "I feel strong."
- Now go through each of the above steps for the rest of your finer energies, moving up through your body, and finish the sequence by speaking the statements below:

> Feel the self-sufficiency of your lower torso flow throughout your body and say, "I am enough."
> Feel the will power and determination of your solar plexus flow throughout your body and say, "I can do it."
> Feel the love and compassion of your heart and say, "I feel loving and open."
> Feel the self-expression and creativity of your throat throughout your body and say, "I can express myself."
> Feel the mental clarity of your mind harmonizing with your body energies and say, "I feel clear."

If you want to understand better just what your finer energies contribute to your voice and your life, try this experiment:

- Contract or collapse each part of your body related to the statements below, allowing that area to feel weak, small, incapable.
- At the same time speak the following statements in a diminished voice, with no energy or vitality:

> For your legs, say, "I feel weak."
> For your lower torso, say, "I'm not enough."
> For your solar plexus, say, "I can't do it."
> For your heart, say, "I feel shielded and closed."
> For your throat, say, "I can't express myself."
> For your mind, say, "I'm confused."

This experiment should help you appreciate the benefits of contacting your positive essential qualities.

As time goes by, you will become more adept at actually hearing these qualities enhance your vocal sound and your self-expression. Surprising as this may seem at first, you will eventually treasure what these energies add to the way you sound. This is an exciting, very special step toward becoming an even more dynamic communicator, with a voice that fully reflects your charisma and aliveness.

Index

211